The Rise and Fall of the Complementarian Doctrine of the Trinity

The Rise and Fall of the Complementarian Doctrine of the Trinity

KEVIN GILES

CASCADE *Books* · Eugene, Oregon

THE RISE AND FALL OF THE COMPLEMENTARIAN DOCTRINE
OF THE TRINITY

Cascade Books
An Imprint of Wipf and Stock Publishers
199 W. 8th Ave., Suite 3
Eugene, OR 97401

www.wipfandstock.com

PAPERBACK ISBN: 978-1-5326-1866-6
HARDCOVER ISBN: 978-1-4982-4443-5
EBOOK ISBN: 978-1-4982-4442-8

Cataloguing-in-Publication data:

Names: Giles, Kevin.

Title: The rise and fall of the complementarian doctrine of the Trinity / Kevin Giles.

Description: Eugene, OR: Cascade Books, 2017 | Includes bibliographical references and index.

Identifiers: ISBN 978-1-5326-1866-6 (paperback) | ISBN 978-1-4982-4443-5 (hardcover) | ISBN 978-1-4982-4442-8 (ebook)

Subjects: LCSH: Trinity—History of doctrines | Jesus Christ—History of doctrines | Evangelicalism | Subordinationism | Sex role—Religious aspects—Christianity | Women—Religious aspects—Christianity

Classification: BT111.3 G545 2017 (print) | BT111.3 (ebook)

Manufactured in the U.S.A.   08/16/17

Contents

Introduction

I have been crying out to complementarians[1] for nearly twenty years, "Go back, you are going the wrong way on the Trinity. What you are teaching in the light of the creeds and confessions is heresy."[2] For well over a decade, I could count on one hand—and have fingers to spare—the theologians who openly supported me.[3] Most evangelicals and Reformed theologians for most of this period in fact opposed me and were very critical of my

1. "Complementarians" are evangelical and Reformed Christians who believe the Bible teaches that in creation God differentiated the sexes on the basis of differing "roles." Men have the "role" of leading in the church and the home, and women, the "role" of submitting. This self-designation was first coined in 1990. So-called complementarians are opposed by evangelical and Reformed Christians who call themselves "egalitarian evangelicals." Egalitarian evangelicals believe that in creation before the fall the two creationally differentiated sexes shared rule. The subordination of women is entirely a consequence of the fall, and is not the God-given ideal. They emphatically affirm the "complementarity" of the sexes. With most other Christians they agree that two sexes "complete" what it means to be human.

2. See my books, *The Trinity and Subordinationism; Jesus and the Father; The Eternal Generation of the Son,* and a dozen scholarly articles in various publications. I do not want to recant anything I said in years past, but my thinking on the Trinity has developed and deepened over the nearly twenty years that I have been working on this profound doctrine. To be fair to my views, quoting a line or two from something I wrote on the Trinity many years ago is not necessarily representative of my more developed thinking about the doctrine of the Trinity.

3. Millard Erickson deserves special mention. Like me he has openly opposed complementarian teaching on the Trinity. To have this prestigious theologian in support was and is wonderful. Nevertheless, I must mention that he has not been entirely supportive. He does not, as I do, affirm the doctrine of the eternal generation of the Son nor unreservedly agree with me on the Trinity. He argues, for example, in his book, *Who's Tampering with the Trinity,* 147–49, that I have Athanasius wrong; at times he does eternally subordinate the Son. On checking his evidence I found it to be incorrect. On this see my *The Eternal Generation of the Son,* 113, note 120.

1

work. I often felt like the boy who cried out, "The King has no clothes on," only to be cuffed around the ears by the princes and courtiers of the King. Slowly evangelical egalitarians began agreeing with me, but complementarians with very few exceptions stood in total opposition. Suddenly and unexpectedly in June 2016 everything changed. A few brave and honest complementarian princes said,[4] "You know the boy is right, the King is naked," and then everyone was free to state the obvious; the hierarchical ordering of the three divine persons is a denial of the creeds and confessions of the church. I now have so many evangelical and Reformed theological friends that I cannot number them.

There can no denying that a revolution has taken place in the complementarian community. The about-turn of Dr. Denny Burk, the president of the Council of Biblical Manhood and Womanhood (CBMW), a long-time dogmatic supporter of the eternal subordination of the Son and of the argument that women's subordination is grounded in the life of God,[5] proves the point. On August 10th, 2016, he broke with his friends Wayne Grudem and Bruce Ware, saying "[I now] do not agree with all their Trinitarian views."[6] Rather, "as a result of what has unfolded over the last two months, I believe in eternal generation, a single divine will, inseparable operations, and the whole Nicene package."[7] And he added that, when putting the complementarian case, appealing to "speculative, extra-biblical Trinitarian analogies . . . is unhelpful and unwarranted in Scripture."[8] And furthermore, "I think it is good and right to leave behind the language of subordination" in reference to Jesus Christ.[9]

Telling the story

In the first chapter of this book, I tell the story of how the complementarian doctrine of a hierarchically ordered Trinity first came to be articulated and how it prospered after a slow start and gained ascendancy in evangelical and

---

4. In the story of how this happened I will tell how in fact two princesses were the first to cry out and then the princes were embolded to cry out also.

5. Burk, "Why the Trinity Must Inform Our Views on Gender."

6. Burk, "My Take Away from the Trinity Debate."

7. Ibid.

8. Ibid.

9. Ibid.

Reformed circles.[10] I make the point that on 1st June 2016 it seemed that the complementarian hierarchical construal of the Trinity had triumphed and virtually all complementarians were agreed that this was the unassailable ground for the hierarchical ordering of the sexes. At this point of time, the complementarians were supremely confident that they had won the debate on the Trinity and that those dangerous "evangelical feminists" who argued for a co-equal Trinity and the substantial equality of the two differentiated sexes, especially Kevin Giles, had been routed and shown to be the heretics.

In chapter 2, I tell how civil war over the doctrine of the Trinity broke out in the complementarian world on 3rd June 2016 and how the forces under Generals Grudem and Ware were defeated. I then explore why this civil war broke out at this time, who the leaders of the revolutionary forces were, and the challenges of reconstruction now facing complementarians after their great defeat. This is a difficult time for them because it would seem that the complementarian hierarchical doctrine of the Trinity now has few supporters. It has been abandoned even by many of its once most ardent supporters and advocates. This defeat undeniably calls into question the complementarian doctrine of the sexes, or at least how it has been articulated by the Council of Biblical Manhood and Womanhood in the Danvers Statement of 1987.[11] Wayne Grudem admits this. He says that for twenty-five years he has believed that how the Trinity is construed "may well turn out to be the most decisive factor in finally deciding" the bitter debate between evangelicals about the status and ministry of women.[12]

In chapter 3 I ask the question, how was it that the majority of evangelical and Reformed theologians came to endorse and teach the complementarian doctrine of a hierarchically ordered Trinity that now many of them judge to be "heresy"? I conclude that the primary reason is that their theological methodology was seriously flawed. Their methodology is encapsulated in the slogan, "All my theology comes directly from Scripture."[13]

---

10. A number of people have critically read sections of this book or the whole book in draft. Rachel Miller and Roland Ward read the whole book. Carl Trueman, Keith E. Johnson, Paul Collier, and Aimee Byrd, read chapters 2 and 3. Robert Letham read and commented on the three sections where I discuss his work.

11. The Danvers Statement.

12. Grudem, *Evangelical Feminism*, 411, note 12.

13. Some who speak this way also say, "we have no creed but the Bible," but this latter slogan is not used in *the New Reformed* movement, which is my heritage, and is now represented by "the Gospel Coalition" and allied groups. I will say more on these matters as the book progresses.

In reply, I outline a better methodology, one followed by the sixteenth-century Reformers and articulated in modern times by the best of confessional Reformed theologians. This gives primacy to Scripture yet acknowledges that working out what is foundational and central in the varied comments in Scripture, or what should be *inferred* from Scripture when it does not speak explicitly on an issue, is not self-evident. This methodology also listens carefully to the doctrinal tradition, authoritatively outlined in creeds and confessions. This informs theologians on what the church in the past has agreed is the teaching of Scripture. And this methodology gives place to reason enlightened by the Spirit in the "doing" of theology.

In chapter 4, in reply to the complementarians who argue that their doctrine of the Trinity springs directly from Scripture, I outline how in fact the doctrine of the Trinity came to be formulated in history. This story shows that the doctrine of the Trinity was hammered out over four centuries and is the outcome of conflict and dispute over what the Bible teaches on the Father-Son relationship, many a wrong turn and bad mistake, and much profound theological reflection. To conclude this chapter, I spell out the Nicene doctrine of the Trinity as it is codified in the creeds and confessions of the church.

Finally, in chapter 5, a short chapter, I sum up what we have learned from telling this story and suggest the agenda that this story now sets for evangelicals as they look to the future.

In what follows, we will hear of the many very harsh things that have been said of those who have opted for a hierarchical doctrine of the Trinity in order to ground the hierarchical ordering of the sexes on the weightiest theology possible. Their critics accuse them of "heresy," "blasphemy," "idolatry," "Arianism," "subordinationism," and of "departing from biblical Christianity." All these stringent accusations have been made by Reformed theologians of complementarian conviction.

The doctrine of the Trinity is the main agenda, not gender

In this book, how the doctrine of the Trinity is rightly articulated is always the issue in focus. In all my writings on the Trinity this has been my primary and central concern. I have simply wanted to expound and defend the creedal and confessional doctrine of the Trinity. In what follows, however, as in my other writings on the Trinity, the debate about the relationship of the sexes often gets mentioned—more often than I wish. It could not be otherwise because the doctrine of the Trinity got corrupted in evangelical and Reformed circles when it was co-opted as the basis for the subordination of women in the mid-1970s and then became integral to what would come to be known after about 1990 as the "complementarian position." Thus, to explain and evaluate what complementarians teach on the Trinity I cannot avoid commenting on what they teach about women, because the two matters are inextricably connected in complementarian theology.

Complementarians almost universally assert that egalitarian evangelicals are the ones who have corrupted the doctrine of the Trinity by arguing that the three divine persons are "co-equal" and thus men and women are "equal."[14] To start with, we see how unconvincing this argument is on noting that the Athanasian Creed says Christians should believe that the three divine persons are "co-equal." If egalitarian Christians speak of the Father, Son, and Spirit as "co-equal" then they are simply reflecting historic orthodoxy! Certainly a few egalitarians have appealed to the Trinity in support of the substantial equality of the creation-differentiated sexes, but such appeals are rare.[15] Virtually every evangelical egalitarian book primarily appeals to Scripture, saying nothing at all about the Trinity. In the definitive summary of the evangelical egalitarian position given by Christians for Biblical Equality (CBE), the Trinity is not mentioned.[16] None of the contributors to the definitive book of essays outlining the evangelical egalitarian case, *Discovering Biblical Equality: Complementarity without Hierarchy*,[17] makes any appeal to the Trinity as the basis for gender equality. Rebecca Groothuis, the co-editor, says that to argue that Christ is eternally "role"-subordinated to the Father, is "rife with logical and theological difficulties [and] utterly fails as an analogy to woman's subordination."[18] My chapter on the Trinity

14. This charge is repeated many times in Ware and Stark's 2015 book, *One God in Three Persons*.

15. The most important evangelical book to make this argument is Grenz and Kjesbo, *Women in the Church*, 151–56. The late Stanley Grenz was a competent theologian and what he and Kjesbo say on the Trinity is very well informed and cannot be easily dismissed. I note, however, that Grenz was a social trinitarian who believed that God's social life in heaven had social implications on earth. I am not a social trinitarian and social trinitarianism today, twenty years after this book was published, is not supported by theologians who argue that fourth-century pro-Nicene teaching on the Trinity should be seen as historic orthodoxy.

16. "Statement on men, women, and equality."

17. Pierce and Groothuis, eds., *Discovering Biblical Equality*.

18. Ibid., 332.

in this book is entirely an argument in opposition to the complementarian doctrine of a hierarchically ordered Trinity, which I claim breaches historic orthodoxy.[19] I have never argued for gender equality by appeal to the Trinity.[20] The complementarian theologian, Fred Sanders, confirms what I say. On his blog and in a personal email to me, he first apologizes for "rough handling" me in opposing my claim that complementarian teaching on the Trinity breaches Nicene orthodoxy and then says, "I have not been able to find one sentence where Kevin Giles works to secure his own [gender] egalitarian position by appeal to the Trinity."[21]

From these comments you should rightly conclude that I do not espouse some distinctive evangelical doctrine of the Trinity, nor do other evangelical egalitarians. I say again, in all my writings on the Trinity I have sought only to accurately articulate the Nicene and confessional doctrine of the Trinity. If any of my critics can show me any instance where I differ from what the church across the centuries has agreed is the teaching of Scripture on the Trinity I will gladly recant. For several decades before 2016, the fact that one's doctrine of the Trinity was not necessarily indicative of one's doctrine of the male-female relationship was not obvious to most evangelicals. What was obvious was that almost all complementarian theologians argued for a hierarchically ordered Trinity and I and a very few other evangelical egalitarians argued against this teaching, claiming it was simply a reworded form of Arianism. Only in mid-2016 did it become clear that the sharp divide over the Trinity among evangelical Christians was not between complementarians and evangelical egalitarians but between those who insisted that the creeds and confessions of the church ruled on how

19. Ibid., 334–54.

20. I have written three small books arguing that the creation ideal is the substantial equality of the sexes: *Women and their Ministry* (1977), *Created Woman* (1985), and, *Better Together* (2010). In the first two I make no appeal to the Trinity and in the last I have an appendix opposing any appeal to the Trinity by either side in this debate. I must admit, nevertheless, that in my big book, *The Trinity and Subordinationism*, published in 2002, I speak warmly of Millard Erickson's social doctrine of the Trinity and of his argument that this has social implications, and I commend others of this opinion as well. This was my first work on the Trinity and when I wrote social trinitarianism was very much in favor. It is to be noted, nevertheless, that even in this book I do not ground male-female equality in the Trinity. In the section of this book in which I put my case for male-female equality as the ideal (194–211), I appeal only to the Bible. In the last ten years or more I have openly and unambiguously argued that the Trinity should not be appealed to by either side in this debate.

21. Sanders, "A Plain Account of Trinity and Gender."

the Scriptures are rightly to be interpreted on the Trinity and other major doctrines and those who believed with Bible in hand they could construe the Trinity independently as individuals.

My unique qualifications

In writing this story I am uniquely positioned and informed. I have been actively involved in the robust debate between egalitarian evangelicals and complementarians for more than forty years. My first book, *Women and their Ministry: A Case for Equal Ministries in the Church Today*, was published in 1977, and my first entry into the debate about the Trinity, *The Trinity and Subordinationism*, was published in 2002. I suspect my arch theological opponent, Dr. Wayne Grudem, is the only person to have written more on these two matters than me. He quotes me often in his books, dismisses me as an "evangelical feminist," and castigates me (in his opinion) for rejecting the authority of Scripture. In his book, *Evangelical Feminism: A New Path to Liberalism*, he gives a whole chapter to listing my sins.[22] I have made many a reply to his writings and accusations.[23]

I am also uniquely positioned and informed to write this book specifically on the complementarian civil war over the Trinity, because arguably my writings on the Trinity, more than the work of anyone else, precipitated this civil war.[24] In support of this audacious claim, I note that when the Evangelical Theological Society (ETS)—with over 4,500 members, most with a PhD—was forced to concede that the complementarian doctrine of the Trinity had been judged heretical by many theologians and the issue had to be got out in the open, I was asked to give the opening address at the plenary forum on the Trinity at the annual ETS conference in San Antonio in November 2016. This was a huge honor. More than 2,500 evangelical theologians come each year to this conference; in 2016 the attendees numbered 2,641. On stage with me where Millard Erickson, Wayne Grudem, and Bruce Ware. Possibly five hundred theologians were present at this forum.[25]

---

22. Pages 115–18.

23. My books and articles on men and women in the Bible and the Trinity, which will be footnoted as the book progresses, establishes this point.

24. I will substantiate this claim in chapter 2 in telling the story of how and why the complementarian doctrine of the Trinity came to be rejected.

25. You can read about what happened at this forum and of my contribution in Woods, "Wayne Grudem Has Changed His Mind on the Trinity."

CHAPTER 1

The Rise and Rise of the Complementarian Doctrine of the Trinity

On 1 June 2016 it seemed that the complementarian hierarchical doctrine of the Trinity had won the day.[1] Most of the best known evangelical and Reformed theologians were either positively advocating or openly supportive of this construal of the Trinity. They were agreed that the hierarchical ordering of the three divine persons was historic orthodoxy; what the creeds and confessions of the church taught and what the best of theologians from the past believed. The few critics, and I was the most published, were dismissed as "evangelical feminists" who were postulating the "co-equality" of the three divine persons to further their own agenda to deny or minimise male-female differentiation. They were the ones in error.

In this chapter I am going to tell when and by whom this complementarian hierarchical doctrine of the Trinity was first devised and made the basis for the traditional ordering of the sexes and how it prospered after a slow start, becoming foundational and integral to what we now call "the complementarian position."

---

1. Complementarians use a number of acronyms to self-designate their position: EFS, the eternal functional subordination of the Son; ERS, the eternal relational subordination of the Son, and ERAS, the eternal relationship of authority and submission. These self-designations make the point that something other than the Nicene doctrine of the Trinity is being promulgated. The words differ in each acronym but the doctrine is one: the Son is eternally set under the authority of the Father. Denny Burk, "My Takeaway from the Trinity Debate," the president of CBMW, writing in the latter part of 2016, says, "One of the results of the recent Trinity debate is that the term 'eternal functional subordination' (EFS) has been substantially redefined. Before this controversy, EFS wasn't one view. It was umbrella terminology for a certain species of views that shared in common the idea that the Son submits to his Father in some qualified sense from all eternity."

The invention of the complementarian doctrine of the Trinity

All new directions in theology are articulated first in a point of time, usually by one person, in most cases a man. The very first person in history to speak of "the role subordination" of women, and of "the eternal role subordination of the Son of God," in both cases meaning in plain English their subordination in authority and nothing else, was George Knight III in his highly influential 1977 book, *New Testament Teaching on the Role Relationship of Men and Women.*[2] In this book, he rejected the historic way of speaking of men as "superior," women "inferior" that had reigned until the middle part of the twentieth century, arguing instead that men and women are "equal," yet "role differentiated." These differing "roles," he said, were given in creation before the fall. As such, they give the God-given ideal and are transcultural and transtemporal. This wording sounded acceptable to the modern ear: who could deny that men and women are different in significant ways and tend to have different roles—women bear and nurture children, do most of the house-work; men do the gardening, cook at Bar-B-Qs, at least in Australia, and watch sport on TV?

For Knight, 1 Corinthians 11:3 is pivotal to his case. He says Paul "begins his argument about the role relationship of men and women [in this passage] by placing it in a hierarchy of headships."[3] He say the Greek word, *kephalē,* translated "head, is used 'to denote superior rank.'"[4] Thus, he concludes that 1 Corinthians 11:3 is speaking of "the authority relationships that God has established between the Father and the Son, the Son and man, and man and woman."[5] He says the text speaks of "a chain of subordination."[6] In descending order of authority stand the Father, Son, man, woman. In making this argument Knight grounded the subordination of women on his conclusion that the persons of the Trinity are hierarchically ordered.

Before Dr. Knight wrote, the modern word "role" had never been used to speak of the essential difference between men and women or of the essential difference between the divine three. Now we see the huge significance

2. Knight, *New Testament Teaching.*

3. Ibid., 32.

4. Ibid., 32, note 6.

5. Ibid, 57, See also 33.

6. Ibid., 33.

9

of his work. This one man produced a way of speaking of the male-female relationship that preserved what he called the "traditional" understanding of male "headship" that sounded acceptable to modern ears and in doing so reworded and redefined the doctrine of the Trinity in the terms he had invented to speak of what he believed was the primary difference between the sexes.

This formulation of the doctrine of the Trinity, I must add, involved far more than just introducing the word "role." Knight also argued that the divine three persons are ordered hierarchically. He spoke of a "chain of subordination."[7] In doing so he openly, but without admitting it, broke with historic orthodoxy. The Athanasian Creed says: "In this Trinity none is before or after the other, none is greater or less than another, . . . the three persons are coequal"; all three are "almighty" and "Lord." The Belgic Confession of 1561 says, "All three [are] co-eternal and co-essential. There is neither first nor last: for they are all three one, in truth, in power, in goodness, and in mercy." The Second Helvetic Confession of 1566 says that the "three persons [are] consubstantial, coeternal, and coequal," and then it condemns those who teach that any divine person is "subservient, or subordinate to another in the Trinity, and that there is something unequal, a greater or less in one of the divine persons." If I wanted to absolutely exclude hierarchical ordering in the Trinity, specifically the eternal subordination of the Son in authority, I could not do better than is done in these documents, which sum up what the church believes the Scriptures teach. Why so few recognized that Knight was teaching a doctrine of the Trinity explicitly excluded by the Athanasian Creed and the Reformation confessions is a question that demands an answer, but I will leave this answer to my readers.

Knight's use of the modern English word "role," which finds its late nineteenth-century origins in the theatre and its early twentieth-century academic usage in humanistic sociology, needs further comment. The word is not found in any of the more common modern translations of the Bible. In dictionary usage and in sociological texts the words "role" and its synonym, "function," speak of routine behavior or acts, and so we ask, for example, who has the role of gardening, washing clothes, doing the shopping, managing the finances, etc., in the home? In this everyday usage it is understood that roles and functions can change and do change. They are not fixed and person-defining. In the novel usage invented by Knight,

7. Knight, *New Testament Teaching*, 33.

10

and now entrenched in the evangelical world, a "role" is given an entirely different meaning found in no dictionary or sociological text. A "role" has nothing to do with routine behavior. It is a person-defining category, speaking of fixed *power relations*, not *role relations* that may change from place to place and from time to time. God the Father and men have the "role" or "function" of leading ("headship"); the Son of God and women have the "role" of submitting—and this can never change. To prove that this so-called "role subordination" does not imply subordination in being or inferiority in person (ontological subordination), carefully chosen illustrations are cited of the ship's captain and the crewman, the officer and the private in an army, and the manager and the worker. In each of these cases, the point is valid. These illustrations of differing "roles" do not imply ontological subordination or personal inferiority because first, the roles can change and second because the higher position/role invariably has some basis in competence, training, age, etc. It is not ascribed by birth. The problem is that these carefully chosen and selective illustrations in fact do not parallel what is being argued. The exact parallels to the distinctive complementarian usage of the terms "function" and "role," introduced by Knight, are to be found in classic aristocracy, race-based slavery, and in apartheid, where one's so-called "role" or "function" is ascribed by birth and it can never change. In this usage, the one who rules is understood to be of a superior class or status and the one who obeys of an inferior class or status. In other words, "difference in role" speaks of an *essential and unchangeable* difference between persons, which is predicated on the premise that some are born to rule and some to obey. The rulers and the ruled are not social equals and never can be. So what Knight and his followers are actually arguing is that the Son and women are defined by their subordination. The word "role" was deliberately chosen by Knight to obfuscate what he was actually arguing, namely that one party is permanently subordinated in authority to another.

When the word "role" is used in this novel sense to speak of what primarily differentiates the Father and the Son, the orthodox doctrine of the Trinity is undermined, if not demolished. This would not be the case if the word were being used to speak only of the differing works or operations of the divine persons, as the dictionary definition suggests, but this is not the case. What is actually being argued is that what primarily differentiates the Father and the Son is differing *authority*: who rules over whom for all eternity. Because this difference is eternal and person-defining it speaks of *ontological* difference. In what I suspect is an authorial slip, Knight openly admits this near the end of his book. He says "the eternal role subordination of the Son" has "ontological" implications.[8]

Why theologians did not cry out in dismay at his novel and (it would seem) deliberately obfuscating use of this non-biblical word, "role", drawn from the theatre and humanistic sociology to redefine trinitarian and gender relations is worrying and problematic. Evangelical egalitarians strongly objected and made devastating critiques that complementarians ignored or dismissed summarily.[9] Only once have I seen a complementarian object to this use of the word "role." Werner Neuer, a German-speaking complementarian and Old Testament scholar, concludes that "in the cause of truth" the word "role" should be abandoned by complementarians.[10]

Before leaving Knight's creative and influential book, I highlight the circular nature of his argument. First, he reformulated the doctrine of the sexes on the basis of differing "roles," by which he means differing authority. Then he reformulated and reworded the doctrine of the Trinity exactly in the same way. Finally, he appealed to his novel doctrine of the Trinity to substantiate his teaching on the sexes. Reading our earthly agenda into the life of God is called "theological projection."

How Knight's hierarchically ordered doctrine of the Trinity came to prevail

Knight's entirely novel reformulation of the case for male "headship" was embraced with gusto by most evangelicals and Reformed theologians, but not by all. In this totally new social context, created by the advent of women's lib, some evangelicals and Reformed theologians began advocating for a radical break from the traditional understanding of the relationship of the sexes. They argued that Genesis chapter 1 and the teaching and example of Jesus, made the substantial equality of the two creation-differentiated sexes the God-given ideal.[11] This generated a healthy and robust debate in

---

8. Ibid., 56. He admits this three times in the first paragraph on this page.

9. So Groothuis, "Equal in Being, Unequal in Role"; Giles, The Genesis of Confusion."

10. Neuer, *Man and Woman*, 30.

11. On the egalitarian side, see the early books, Scanzoni and Hardesty, *All We're Meant to Be;* Jewett, *Man as Male and Female,* and Giles, *Women and Their Ministry,* and there were many others. I speak of the *"substantial* equality" of the sexes to differentiate this position from the complementarian one that affirms only the spiritual or

the evangelical world beginning in the mid 1970s and ending in the late 1980s. One side called themselves "traditionalists" or "hierarchicalists" and the other side called themselves "egalitarians" or "evangelical egalitarians." These respectful though sometimes heated debates were common in the USA, England, Canada, and Australia at this time. The debate was almost entirely about what the Bible taught on the male-female relationship. The Trinity was not as a general rule mentioned by either side. I took part in several of these debates in Australia, in print and in public forums, and I cannot remember the Trinity even being mentioned. This observation is confirmed by the Danvers Statement of 1987,[12] which enunciates the case for the permanent subordination of women in the way Knight had formulated it. This document does not mention the Trinity. This date, 1987 marks the end of the healthy and robust debate among evangelical and Reformed Christians about *what the Bible teaches on the man-woman relationship* that I have just discussed. This debate came to an abrupt halt at this point of time because the authors of the Danvers Statement claimed that what they were teaching was what the Bible teaches. From then on, in the minds of those who embraced this statement, those who argued otherwise indicated that they denied biblical authority. What this meant is that evangelical egalitarians were ruled out of court before they could even open their Bibles.

Following the publication of the Danvers Statement, came the definitive study in 1991 setting out the complementarian position, *Recovering Biblical Manhood and Womanhood: A Response to Biblical Feminism.*[13] In the preface to this book, the editors, John Piper and Wayne Grudem, say their "primary purpose"[14] in publishing these essays is to put the case for the "unique leadership role for men in the family and in the church."[15] I say nothing about the various essays; I simply note three things relevant to the story I am telling of how the complementarian position emerged and developed. First, we learn that by 1991 the use of the modern word "role" to speak euphemistically of the differing authority of men and women that Knight first introduced had prevailed. No word is used more often in this

soteriological equality of the sexes. For egalitarians, the concept of equality must have some substance to it.

12. The Danvers Statement.

13. Piper and Grudem, *Recovering Biblical Manhood and Womanhood*. See my review of this book (Giles, Review of *Recovering Biblical*).

14. Ibid., xiv.

15. Ibid., xii. I italicize the word "role."

book. Second, a new word to designate the case for the Danver's position had been "coined." In their preface to the book, Piper and Grudem say they are "uncomfortable" with the common designations of their position, "traditional" or "hierarchical." They propose a new self-designate for what they teach, the "complementarian" position.[16] This self-designation simply confuses the debate. For at least ten years previously egalitarian evangelicals had been describing the male-female relationship as "complementary," as they still do with enthusiasm.[17] Third, this book confirms what I said above about Knight's Trinity argument gaining little traction in the late 1970s and the 1980s. In *Recovering Biblical Manhood and Womanhood*, the Trinity argument is mentioned just eleven times in over 500 pages in only five of the twenty-six chapters. This argument is known, found in several chapters and endorsed by the editors, but it is obviously at this time not integral or central to the complementarian position.

Wayne Grudem

With the publication of Wayne Grudem's *Systematic Theology: An Introduction to Biblical Doctrine* in 1994, the Trinity argument for the first time became integral to the complementarian position. He gives a full chapter to the doctrine of the Trinity in which he argues in detail for the eternal subordination of the Son.[18] He makes this the ultimate basis for the permanent subordination of women. And he gives a full chapter to the relationship of the sexes, which is basically an exposition of his case for "male headship."[19] In this chapter, he argues that the hierarchical ordering of the sexes on earth is predicated on the hierarchical ordering of the divine three persons in eternity.[20] He is emphatic that what he is teaching on these matters is what the Bible teaches and what the church has always believed.

In his chapter on the Trinity, in the first twenty-two pages (226–48), Grudem gives a clear and well set out summary of the orthodox doctrine of the Trinity and its biblical basis, and a good account of the various trinitarian heresies. The one thing that caught my attention on these pages was his

16. Piper and Grudem, *Recovering*, xiv. I tell this story in full in Giles, "Genesis of Confusion."

17. I give the evidence for this assertion in my "Genesis of Confusion."

18. *Recovering*, 226–61.

19. Ibid., 454–71.

20. Ibid., 459.

frequent appeals to the family analogy, rather than to Scripture, to explain the Father-Son relationship.[21] I only realized the significance of this when I came to pages 248–57, where Grudem discusses "the distinctions between the Father, the Son, and the Holy Spirit." In these pages he breaks with historic orthodoxy. For him, what primarily distinguishes and differentiates the three divine persons, especially the Father and the Son, is differing authority.[22] He says, the Father uniquely has "the role of commanding, directing, and sending," and the Son has the role of "obeying, going as the Father sends, and revealing God to us."[23] Later, when speaking of how the Trinity prescribes the male-female relationships, he says, "The Father has greater authority. He has a leadership role among all the members of the Trinity that the Son and the Spirit do not have."[24] Quoting 1 Corinthians 11:3, he says,

> Paul makes the parallel explicit when he says, "I want you to understand that the head of every man is Christ, the head of woman is her husband, and the head of Christ is God. Here is a distinction in authority. . . .
>
> Just as God the Father has authority over the Son, though the two are equal in deity, so in marriage, the husband has authority over his wife, though they are equal in personhood. In this case, the man's role is like that of God the Father, and the woman's role is parallel to that of God to the Son.[25]

The outcome of this teaching is that we end up with a doctrine of the Trinity where the divine three persons are hierarchically ordered; the Father eternally rules over the Son, and this is the basis for the hierarchical ordering of the sexes.

---

21. Ibid., 230, 232, 241, 243, 247.

22. Ibid., 251. He says, if we do not have "subordination then there is no inherent difference in the way the three divine persons relate to one another, and consequently we do not have three distinct persons." In his later book, *Evangelical Feminism*, 433, he says, "the differences in authority among the Father, Son, and Holy Spirit are the only interpersonal differences that the Bible indicates that exist *eternally* among the members of the Godhead," and, "if we did not have such differences in authority in relationships among the members of the Trinity, then we would not know of any differences at all."

23. Grudem, *Systematic Theology*, 250.

24. Ibid, 459.

25. Ibid., 459–60.

Grudem quotes many texts, most of them highlighted by Arius, that may imply or do speak of the subordination of the Son.[26] Like Arius, he concludes that the titles, "the Father" and "the Son," indicate that the Bible teaches the eternal subordination of the Son. These titles disclose that the Father is a real father and the Son a real son. Fathers rule over sons and sons obey. I have already made the point that in his account of historic trinitarian orthodoxy Grudem frequently appeals to a family analogy to explain the Father-Son relationship. The importance of this observation becomes apparent on pages 248–57, where his teaching on the Trinity most clearly parts from historic orthodoxy. Here he says,

> The Father and the Son relate to one another as a father and a son relate to one another in a human family; the father directs and has authority over the son, and the son obeys and is responsive to the directions of the father. The Holy Spirit is obedient to the directives of both the Father and the Son.[27]

And then pushing the human analogy even further he says,

> The gift of children within a marriage, coming from both the father and the mother, and subject to the authority of the father and the mother, is analogous to the relationship of the Holy Spirit to the Father and the Son in the Trinity.[28]

On reading this comment, the confessional Reformed gender complementarian Todd Pruitt said I could "barely keep my mind from spinning."[29] Grudem's words go "beyond reasonable speculation. In an effort to be charitable I want to call it *exotic*. But this will not do. It is worse than exotic. It may well be blasphemous."

And then he says,

> The stubborn insistence of Drs Ware and Grudem to force a parallel between the Father and the Son, to a husband and a wife is worse than troubling. And we can see from the passage cited above, it leads to the inevitable comparison of the Holy Spirit to the child of the divine husband (Father) and wife (Son). These

---

26. No one denies some texts do this. Nicene orthodoxy insists that such texts speak of the *self-chosen* subordination of the Son *in his incarnation*, as taught in Philippians 2:4–11.

27. Ibid., 249.

28. Ibid., 257.

29. "A mythological Godhead", July 9, 2016, http://www.alliancenet.org/mos/1517/a-mythological-godhead#.WRbKgu6GOUk.

> parallels have far more in common with pagan mythology than Biblical Theology. . . . This is a distortion of the Godhead and there is nothing helpful or beautiful about it.

I thoroughly agree with Pruitt. Grudem and Ware's characteristic depiction of God's threefold life in heaven in human terms is thoroughly objectionable. Instead of appealing to Scripture to define divine triune relations, these theologians appeal to fallen creaturely relationships. The divine Father is likened to a human father, the Son to a wife and mother and the Spirit to a child created by his human parents. In this "theology" the Son is feminized and divine relations are sexualized. What we evangelicals should do is appeal to Scripture for our understanding of divine life and relations. In the Bible the Father, the Son and the Spirit are all God in all might, majesty, glory and power. They are depicted as unlike human beings.

The impact of Grudem's *Systematic Theology* on evangelical and Reformed Christians—particularly young, mostly male, theological students—cannot be overestimated. It is the most widely used theology text in evangelical and Reformed seminaries and Bible Colleges around the world. More than 500,000 copies have been sold and the book has been translated into eight languages and eight other translations are in progress. He is emphatic that the *eternal subordination of the Son in authority* stands right at the heart of the orthodox doctrine of the Trinity. More than anyone else he has led the majority of evangelical and Reformed Christians to accept as orthodoxy an Arian-like hierarchical doctrine of the Trinity, where the Son is eternally subordinated to the Father.

Following the publication of his *Systematic Theology*, Grudem published a seemingly unending stream of articles and books where he honed, developed, and promulgated his complementarian doctrine of the Trinity and the sexes.[30] In these works he consistently argues that,

1. The Bible clearly teaches the eternal subordination in authority of the Son. The Father sends the Son and because he is a son, like any human son, he must obey his Father.

---

30. Grudem, *Evangelical Feminism and Biblical Truth*; Grudem, *Evangelical Feminism: A New Path to Liberalism*; Grudem, *Countering the Claims of Evangelical Feminism*; Grudem, "Biblical Evidence for the Eternal Submission"; Grudem, "Whose Position Is Really New?"; Grudem, "Doctrinal Deviations;" Grudem, "Another Thirteen Evangelical Theologians Who Affirm the Eternal Submission of the Son", and this list is not exhaustive.

2. The Bible clearly predicates the subordination of women on the subordination of the Son in 1 Corinthians 11:3. In this text, *kephalē*/head, means "head over"/"authority over."

3. The eternal subordination of the Son and the subordination of women is what the church has always believed.

4. The best of theologians have consistently taught the eternal subordination of the Son. This is historic orthodoxy.

5. Anyone who is of another opinion is a liberal who rejects biblical authority and denies what orthodoxy teaches on the Trinity.

To give weight to his doctrine of the Trinity, Grudem claims that many of the best-known evangelical and Reformed theologians teach what he teaches. In a recent publication, he lists eighteen evangelical theologians who he thinks agree with him.[31] Eight of them are post-Knight complementarians (Packer, Reymond, Ware, Geisler, Ryrie, Yarnell, Frame, and Ovey), and a ninth, Letham, is a gender complementarian who has a few careless sentences when he seeks to relate women's subordination to the Son's submission, but theologically he rejects hierarchical ordering in divine life.[32] None of the other ten ever mention, let alone endorse, the *eternal "role" subordination* of the Son. The word "role" was not used in trinitarian discourse before Knight. Calvin and Edwards, most scholars agree, reject the eternal subordination of the Son. Berkhof and Strong are well-informed trinitarian theologians. Any careful reading of their work shows that they too oppose the eternal subordination of the Son, albeit even if they carelessly use the word "subordination," probably only in relation to the Son's work in history. Hodge does teach the subordination of the Son in "rank," but not in "role."[33] Schaff, Bromiley, Henry, and Vos certainly speak of the subordination of the Son, but they say so little on the Trinity we cannot be sure of their views. Lastly, I make the point that for Grudem to list theologians who contradict the creeds and confessions does not make his doctrine orthodoxy! Those who do support him, if they reject the teaching of the creeds and confessions, are also in error.

For most evangelicals, ill-informed on the doctrine of the Trinity and with little interest in the creeds and confessions of the church, Grudem's

31. Grudem, "Another Thirteen Evangelical Theologians."

32. I will be discussing Letham's writings on the Trinity in detail later in this chapter and in the next chapter.

33. See further on Hodge, Giles, *Jesus and the Father*, 35–37.

arguments seemed compelling. His analogical argument—i.e., the Son is like a human son and thus must obey his father—appeared to be irrefutable. It is not. The best of theologians across the ages are almost universally agreed that human terms used of God and human creaturely relationships cannot and should not be understood literally—or to use the technical term, "univocally"—when applied to God the Creator. To do so is to fall into idolatry by defining God in creaturely terms. How most evangelical and Reformed theologians did not immediately recognize this is very worrying. This move to define the Son of God in terms of human sons, rather than in the light of what Scripture says, should be categorically rejected by evangelicals. In the New Testament, the title "the Son" when used of Jesus Christ speaks of his royal status and power, never his subordination. The Son reigns as Lord.

Bruce Ware

Bruce Ware, Professor of Systematic Theology at the Southern Baptist Theological Seminary, is another evangelical theologian who must be mentioned in telling the story of how the complementarian hierarchical doctrine of the Trinity gained ascendancy in the evangelical world. He had long been a protagonist for the complementarian position when he shot to prominence and fame in 2005 with the publication of his monograph, *Father, Son, and Holy Spirit: Relationships, Roles, and Relevance*,[34] which is his account of the doctrine of the Trinity. This book was given glowing endorsements by some of the most respected evangelical leaders. For example, Paige Patterson, President of Southwestern Baptist Theological Seminary, wrote, "[This book] is a remarkable accomplishment of one of the finest scholars in the land." Joseph Stowell, the President of Moody Bible College, said,

> Thanks to the clear thinking and biblically solid perspective of my friend, Bruce Ware, we are now blessed with this stimulating and edifying description of our God who is worthy of wonder and awe. Here is theology that will launch your heart in worship—as all good theology should.

While Randy Stinson, Executive Director of Christians for Biblical Manhood and Womanhood (CBMW), said,

---

34. Ware, *Father, Son, and Holy Spirit.*

I am thrilled to finally have a resource that will help the person in the pew understand how to properly articulate the doctrine [of the Trinity]. Bruce Ware has brilliantly demonstrated that the manner in which the members of the Trinity relate to one another has direct impact on marriage, parenting, work relationships, and more.[35]

In *Father, Son and Holy Spirit*, time and time again Dr Ware speaks of the "supremacy" of the Father and often of his "priority" and "pre-eminence" in the Godhead.[36] For him, the divine persons are not "co-equal" as orthodoxy with one voice asserts. They are "hierarchically" ordered.[37] Thus we are not surprised that he argues that the Father and the Son differ in glory. He says, the Father has "the ultimate and supreme glory";[38] "the ultimate supremacy and highest glory,"[39] and "the highest honor."[40] For this reason, the Son must give "ultimate and highest glory to his Father."[41] In asserting this he contradicts Scripture, which says the Father and the Son are alike to be glorified (1 Cor 2:8; Gal 1:3–5; Eph 1:3–5; Heb 1:3; Rev 5:12–13; 7:9–12, etc), and the Nicene Creed, which says the divine three persons "together" [are to be] "worshipped and glorified," and the Evangelical Theological Society's doctrinal statement, which demands that it members believe that the Father, Son, and Spirit are "equal in power and glory."

Ware characteristically speaks of what eternally and indelibly differentiates the Father and the Son in terms of differing "roles," meaning, differing authority, but at times he allows this has ontological implications. Thus he says, "the authority–submission structure [within the life of God] marks *the very nature of the eternal Being* of the one who is three."[42] The ontological implications of these words cannot be missed. The "very nature" and "eternal Being" of the divine three persons determines "the rightful place each has." In these words he is admitting that the divine three persons do not simply have different functions or roles. Who they *are* is defined by their *nature* and *being* and this is what differentiates

---

35. These three quotes are taken from the back cover of this book.

36. Ibid., 46, 47, 48, 50, 51, 55, 59, 65, 79, etc.

37. Ibid., 21, 72, 79, 157.

38. Ibid., 50.

39. Ibid., 50, 65.

40. Ibid., 55.

41. Ibid., 67, 55.

42. Ibid., 21.

them. If this is the case then the Father and the Son are not one in being (*homoousios*) as the Nicene Creed teaches.

Ontological implications in Ware's teaching on the Trinity also come into view in his discussion of 1 Corinthians 11:3. He argues that in this text Paul clearly teaches that the Father has authority over the Son for all eternity and that husbands have authority over their wives, the former being the basis for the latter. He says,

> 1 Corithians 11:3 offers a truth-claim about the relationship between the Father and the Son that reflects an eternal veracity. That God is the head of Christ is not presented here as an ad hoc relationship for Christ's mission during his incarnation. It is rather stated as an absolute fact regarding this relationship. God is the head of Christ. The Father has authority over the Son. There is a relationship of authority and submission *in the very Godhead* on which other authority and submission relationships of Christ and man, and man and woman depend. The *taxis* [order] of God's headship over his Son accounts for the presence of a *taxis* in man's relationship with Christ and the woman's relationship with man.[43]

I put in italics the words "the very Godhead" because "the very Godhead" is the ontological or immanent Trinity: God as he is for all eternity.

Ware consistently speaks of the eternal "submission" of the Son. He does so following Robert Letham and Scott Horrell, complementarian theologians who warn of the danger of using the word "subordination."[44] Grudem, as we have noted, openly speaks of "the eternal subordination" of the Son and he sees no need to change. He calls this variation in terminology a "minor difference."[45] I agree with him completely. All we have here is two possible English renderings of the one Greek word *hypotassō*. If the Son is eternally and necessarily submissive to the Father then he is eternally and necessarily *subordinate* to the Father.

This book rocketed Ware into stardom. In the complementarian world he joined Grudem to become one of the great champions of the "orthodox" doctrine of the Trinity that those dangerous "evangelical feminists" were bent on denying, pre-eminently Kevin Giles and Millard Erickson.

---

43. Ibid., 77. He says much the same on page 72.

44. In what follows I am drawing on Grudem's essay, "Biblical Evidence for the Eternal Submission of the Son," in Jowers and House, *The New Evangelical Subordinationism*, 223–61.

45. Ibid., 225.

In what I have said so far, I have spoken synonymously of the distinctive "complementarian" or "hierarchical" doctrine of the Trinity. I would argue that an equally accurate descriptive title for this construal of the Trinity would be the Knight-Grudem-Ware doctrine of the Trinity.

Robert Letham

Possibly the most interesting supporter of the thesis that God's triune life in heaven somehow informs the male-female relationship on earth is Dr. Robert Letham.[46] In his 2004 book, *The Holy Trinity in Scripture, History, Theology, and Worship*,[47] we find a comprehensive and informed historical account of the development of the Trinity in which the contribution of all the more important theologians is discussed. In the first 390 pages of his book he gives an accurate and full account of the Nicene doctrine of the Trinity. I agree completely with his conclusion that the essence of the Arian heresy is the "hierarchical" ordering of the divine persons.[48] In these 390 pages I would not want to dissent from anything he says. However, towards the end of the book, when the issue of the male-female relationship comes into view on pages 389–404 (and in his reprinted review of my book, *The Trinity and Subordinationism*, on pages 489–96), we meet another Dr. Letham; a Dr. Letham who speaks of an "obedience"[49] of the Son that is not limited to the economy, and of "the submission of the Son eternally."[50] His language is restrained and careful, but virtually every complementarian has concluded that in these pages he is explicitly supporting their hierarchical doctrine of the Trinity. In my extended review of his book in the *Evangelical Quarterly* I accuse him of putting forward "two views on the Trinity."[51]

Why he virtually contradicts what he has said previously in his book in these few pages he makes plain. He says he digresses to counter the "feminist" theologians, and he names me along with others in a footnote,[52] who

---

46. I sent this section and the two sections later in the book where I interact with Dr. Letham to him, asking for his critical comment. We regularly correspond. I have altered a few words in this section at his request.

47. Letham, *The Holy Trinity*. See Giles, "Review of *The Holy Trinity*, by Robert Letham."

48. Letham, *The Trinity*, 147, 383, 400, 484.

49. Ibid., 392–96.

50. Ibid., 398.

51. Giles, "Review of *The Holy Trinity*, by Robert Letham."

52. Letham, *The Trinity* 392, note 33.

seek "to eliminate anything appearing to give credence to submission by the Son to the Father in the Trinity."[53] In his reprinted review of my book, *The Trinity and Subordinationism,* in appendix 2, he commends my work "as a powerfully written and often compelling argument,"[54] and thanks me for warning him of the dangers of speaking of "the eternal subordination of the Son."[55] However, he accuses me of "troubling modalist tendencies" (along with T. F. Torrance!),[56] and of denying "that the Son submits to the Father in eternity."[57] Again he argues all my theological failings are due to my dangerous argument that the creation ideal is the co-equality of the differentiated sexes, but he words my position in emotive and loaded terms that in no way reflect my views.

Because of his earned stature as a learned theologian, Letham's support of the complementarian doctrine of the Trinity has been hugely significant. He has given legitimation to their construal of the Trinity. He is frequently cited in complementarian literature as endorsing the hierarchical ordering of the divine three persons and as someone who thinks Kevin Giles is the heretic.[58] I must have been told a hundred times, if the learned Dr. Letham disagrees with you, you must be wrong. Complementarians completely ignore the 390 pages where Letham accurately sets out the orthodox doctrine of the Trinity, seeing only the few pages where he endorses "the submission of the Son eternally" and "that the Son submits to the Father in eternity."

What we learn from Dr. Letham is that the minute the doctrine of the Trinity and the relationship of the sexes get mixed up, good theology goes out the door. He and Grudem are miles apart theologically,[59] but when the

---

53. Ibid., 392.

54. Ibid., 490.

55. Ibid., 493.

56. Ibid., 494.

57. Ibid., 495.

58. In complementarian writings he is invariably quoted as a supporter of their hierarchical doctrine of the Trinity. In Ware and Stark's book, *One God,* he is quoted in support six times (11, note 1, 157, 162, 166, 170, 270). In Jowers and House, *The New Evangelical Subordinationism,* he is quoted in support eight times (29, note 15, 35, 150, 224, 225, 226, 295, 348). In the list of theologians that Grudem thinks teach what he teaches, he lists Robert Letham. See, Grudem, "Another Thirteen Evangelical Theologians."

59. Thus, we note that Grudem is a key player in the Evangelical Theological Society and one-time president. Letham, as a confessional Reformed theologian, thinks this organization is theologically defective and has not joined it.

issue of the status and ministry of women comes into view, at least until very recently,[60] Letham agrees with Grudem and defends him.[61]

Complementarians agree, the persons of the Trinity are hierarchically ordered, and this is the ground for hierarchical ordering of the sexes

From the time in 1994 when Grudem published his *Systematic Theology* until June 2016, self-designated complementarians almost uniformly argued that the Son is eternally subordinated, or submissive, to the Father, and that this is the primary ground for the subordination of women. For complementarians, the eternal subordination of the Son in authority and the permanent subordination of women were two sides of the one coin. Their argument was that for those who stood under the authority of Scripture, this is what should be believed because this is what Scripture taught. Knight first made this connection appealing to 1 Corinthians 11:3 as proof, and we saw exactly the same thing in Grudem and Ware's writings. Denny Burk, the current president of the Council for Biblical Manhood and Womanhood, writing in 2013, expressed this opinion very bluntly and strongly. He says the,

> analogy between gender roles and Trinity derives not from mere speculation, but from the Bible. The central text in this regard is 1 Corinthians 11:3:
>
> *But I want you to understand that Christ is the head of every man, and the man is the head of a woman, and God is the head of Christ.*
>
> . . . First Corinthians 11:3 explicitly links the *masculine-feminine dynamic to the Father-Son dynamic.* The apostle Paul himself invokes the analogy, and our challenge is to understand it and receive it. It's a debate worth having precisely because the link between intratrinitarian relations and gender relations is transparently biblical.[62]

This argument, that 1 Corinthians 11:3 hierarchically orders the Father-Son and male-female relationship and links the two, is worked out

60. I will discuss his recent change of mind in the next chapter.

61. See for example, Letham "Reply to Kevin Giles," 341–43.

62. Burk, "Why the Trinity Must Inform Our Views on Gender."

in even more detail and care in Kyle Claunch's chapter, "God is the Head of Christ" in the 2015 book *One God in Three Persons*, edited by Bruce Ware and John Starke.[63] For Claunch, 1 Corinthians 11:3 proves that "male headship as conceived by complementarians is rooted in *the very triune being* of God."[64] Thus, again we have a complementarian arguing that Scripture itself inextricably connects women's subordination and the subordination of the Son in the immanent Trinity and quoting 1 Corinthians 11:3 to substantiate this claim.

After June 2016, when civil war broke out among complementarians over the Trinity, surprisingly leaders of the complementarian movement began saying that belief in the eternal subordination of the Son has never been intrinsic to the complementarian position. This is simply not true, at least from 1994 to 2015. The consensus was that Scripture itself grounded the subordination of women in the subordination of the Son and 1 Corinthians 11:3 was quoted as proof. Denny Burk made this point eloquently, "the link between intratrinitarian relations and gender relations is transparently biblical."[65]

This was the unqualified position of the Council for Biblical Manhood and Womanhood and its president, Owen Strachan, until mid 2016.[66] A number of weighty evangelical systematic theologies subsequent to Grudem's, also argued on the basis of Scripture that the Son is eternally subordinated to the Father and that this is the primary ground for the subordination of women,[67] and a never-ending stream of journal articles and books put this case.[68] It seemed to everyone that complementarians were of one mind. The Bible teaches that the Son is eternally subordinated in authority to the Father and the Bible makes this hierarchical ordering of the divine persons prescriptive for the male-female relationship.

---

63. *One God*, 65–93. Appeal to 1 Corinthians 11:3 is also made in this book by other authors. See pp. 13, 92, 93, 108.

64. Ibid., 81. See also 78, 82, 85, 88. Italics added.

65. Burk, "Why the Trinity Must Inform Our Views on Gender."

66. See Byrd, "What Denny Burk Should Do," and Strachan and Peacock, *The Grand Design*, particularly 75, 93.

67. E.g., Geisler, *Systematic Theology*, 2, 290–91; Frame, *The Doctrine of God*, 719–22; Frame, *Systematic Theology*, 501–2; Reymond, *A New Systematic Theology*, 336; Bird, *Evangelical Theology*, 120.

68. I give a representative list of these publications in my *Jesus and the Father*, 20–32. Later articles and works are found in Jowers and House, *The New Evangelical Subordinationism*. Strachan and Peacock's, *The Grand Design* is the last to be published.

Harvest time beginning in mid-2015

The year from 1 May 2015 to 30 May 2016 was something like a time of harvest for complementarian trinitarian theology. After more than twenty years of arguing for the eternal subordination or submission of the Son it seemed that the rewards of all their work had come to fruition. In this one year, four major studies endorsing hierarchical ordering in divine life were published by evangelicals.

First off the press on 30 April 2015 was Ware and Starke's book, *One God in Three Persons*.[69] It is a collection of essays on the Trinity by complementarian theologians. Like all collections of essays there is diversity of thought and standard. In their preface, Ware and Starke write of the appeal to the Trinity by some liberal scholars and evangelicals (and I am footnoted),[70] who attempt

> to eliminate anything appearing to give credence to the Son's submitting to the Father from eternity. They thereby give ontological reinforcement to a completely egalitarian relationship between male and female.[71]

In response to this dangerous practice, Ware and Starke tell us they write to counter

> the rise of feminism in the church primarily by arguing for a complementarian structure to gender and the local church, but also by appealing to the Trinity.[72]

In saying this, the editors openly admit that their agenda is exactly the agenda they accuse evangelical egalitarians of pursuing: making trinitarian relations in heaven prescriptive for male-female relations on earth.

In reply, first let me say, I and virtually all informed evangelical egalitarians do *not* appeal to the Trinity to support our belief that the Bible makes the substantial equality of the sexes the creation-given ideal.[73] The

69. See my "An Extended Review of *One God in Three Persons*," and the slightly extended edition of it in *Preserving the Trinity*, 16–25.

70. No one is quoted more often in this book.

71. Ware and Starke (eds.), *One God*, 12.

72. Ibid.

73. I outline the evidence for this in the introduction to this book. I am of course aware that a few evangelical egalitarians have appealed to the Trinity as the basis for male-female equality. My point is that this argument is not characteristic or basic to the egalitarian position, indeed, it is rare. Virtually all the better-known and most published

undeniable truth is, as the editors of *One God in Three Persons* makes crystal clear, appealing to the Trinity as a model for gender relations is a distinctive complementarian agenda. For them, a hierarchically ordered Trinity prescribes hierarchically ordered gender relations.[74]

In *One God in Three Persons*, the word "hierarchical" is used repeatedly to describe the divine Father-Son relationship. There is no ambiguity about how the Trinity is construed. However, what struck me most forcibly as I read this book was that most of the contributors appealed directly to the Bible for their doctrine of the Trinity. The creeds and confessions of the church that define what the Bible teaches on the Trinity for the vast majority of Christians in the world gets no hearing at all. For Cowan, John's sending of the Son by the Father and his emphasis that the Son is the son of the Father is illustrative of "John's ubiquitous depiction of a hierarchical relationship between" the Father and the Son.[75] For Clyde Claunch, 1 Corinthians 11:3 proves that "male headship as conceived by complementarians is rooted in the very triune being of God."[76] For James Hamilton, 1 Corinthians 15:2–28 settles matters. For Paul, the Son is ontologically equal with the Father yet eternally subordinate in role.[77] These three chapters, and the one's by Grudem and Ware, imply that with Bible in hand one can formulate the doctrine of the Trinity. That the doctrine of the Trinity actually was worked out in *history* and that the Nicene doctrine of the Trinity is a development of what is *implicit* in Scripture is not recognized, and is in effect denied.

There are nevertheless two chapters in this book that look back to the history of the development of the doctrine of the Trinity, but unfortunately they get it all wrong. John Starke's chapter discusses Augustine's doctrine of the Trinity. He argues that Augustine teaches an "irreversible" "order of authority and submission" between the Father and the Son.[78] I have carefully

---

evangelical egalitarians appeal to the Bible, not the Trinity, for their case that the substantial equality of the sexes is the creation-given ideal. The subordination of women is entirely a consequence of the fall; it is not good, and it is not endorsed by Jesus Christ, who said not one word on "male headship" and much to the contrary. See further my article, "The Genesis of Equality."

74. Claunch, "God is the Head of Christ," in *One God*, makes this point many times. See pages 64, 67, 81, 85, 87, 88, 93.

75. Cowan, "I Always Do What Pleases Him," *One God*, 48.

76. Claunch, "God is the Head of Christ," *One God*, 81.

77. Hamilton, "That God May Be All in All," *One God*, 105, 106, 107, 108.

78. Starke, "Augustine and His Interpreters," *One God*, 170, 171, 172.

read Augustine's *The Trinity,* and several studies by scholars of Augustine's teaching on the Trinity, and I am sure Starke gets Augustine dead wrong. The scholarly consensus is that Augustine's aim is to exclude all forms of subordinationism. Michael Ovey, in his chapter, also appeals to historical sources, mainly Arian creeds of the middle of the fourth century, to prove that "the Father-Son relationship features a relation of superordination and submission" that is eternal.[79] What is breathtaking about Ovey's chapter is that he is an ordained Anglican minister who has given assent to the three creeds and the Thirty-Nine Articles, yet he ignores and denies what these documents say, choosing rather to endorse the teaching of *Arian* creeds.

There is one exception in this book that I must mention, the chapter by Dr. Robert Letham.[80] He does appeal to the creeds and to some of the most significant theologians from the past in his putting the case in support of the doctrine of the eternal generation, a doctrine that Ware and Grudem deny.

One God in Three Persons was enthusiastically received by complementarians and got many very positive endorsements and reviews. John M. Frame, J. D. Trimble Chair of Systematic Theology and Philosophy, Reformed Theological Seminary, Orlando, says, "I find it [the book, *One God*] thoroughly persuasive and I hope it plays a major role in both theological and social discussions."[81] Dr. Sam Storms, the President of the Evangelical Theological Society, says, "this profoundly insightful book is a major contribution to our understanding of the nature of Tri-unity in God."[82] When Stephen Holmes raised question about the book, Fred Sanders, sprang to its defence.[83] Dr. Jared Moore, in his review of this book, written for the Southern Baptist Convention website, says,

> The editors and contributors succeeded in their goal of providing a comprehensive argument from Scripture, history, theological perspective, and philosophy concerning immanent hierarchy among Trinitarian relations. With around 250 pages of content, I do not believe a word was wasted, and the arguments are persuasive.

79. Ovey, "True Sonship," *One God,* 153, cf. 132.

80. Letham, "Eternal Generation in the Church Fathers," *One God,* 109–26.

81. Frame, Review comment, *One God in Three Persons,* https://www.crossway.org/books/one-god-in-three-persons-tpb/.

82. Storms, Review comment, *One God in Three Persons,* https://www.crossway.org/books/one-god-in-three-persons-tpb/.

83. Sanders, "Generations Eternal and Current."

And he adds,

> If complementarians can prove that there is a hierarchy in the immanent (ontological) Trinity, *then they win*, for if a hierarchy exists among the Three Persons of God, and these Three Persons are equally God, then surely God can create men and women equal yet with differing roles in the church and home. . . . [In this book the contributors argue] persuasively that there is hierarchy in the immanent Trinity.[84]

Except for my extended critical review of *One God in Three Persons*,[85] and shorter ones by Stephen Holmes[86] and Rachel Miller,[87] I can find *no* books or articles critical of the contents of the book. Leading evangelical and Reformed theologians enthusiastically welcomed its arrival.

Following the publication of this book, an impressive list of other books on the Trinity, written by evangelical and Reformed theologians, followed in the next twelve months, all arguing for the eternal subordination or submission of the Son and connecting this with the subordination of women.

First came Rodrick K. Durst's book published in November 2015, *Reordering the Trinity: Six Movements of God in the New Testament*.[88] He is Professor of Historical Theology at Golden Gate Baptist Theological Seminary. Durst highlights the fact that in the New Testament the three divine persons are mentioned in close proximity more than seventy times. He notes that in these passages each of the six possible sequential orders are given and that sometimes the Father is mentioned first, sometimes the Son, and sometimes the Spirit. He then seeks to categorise the six sequential orders of the persons, arguing that each sequence indicates a "core theme," such as the "missional," or the "Christological," or the "ecclesial" theme. On this he did not convince me. I can see no self-evident and convincing way to categorise these triadic passages.

One thing he and I agree on completely is that in speaking of the divine three persons the writers of the New Testament frequently do not put the Father "first." However, contrary to his demonstration of this fact, Durst concludes the Father is "first." The Son is eternally "submissive" to

---

84. Moore, "The Complementarians Win."

85. Giles, "An Extended Review of *One God*."

86. Holmes, "Reflections on a New Defence."

87. Miller, "Continuing Down This Path Complementarians Lose."

88. Durst, *Reordering the Trinity*.

the Father. He says, that to argue that the Son is submissive does not imply his ontological subordination.[89] This would be true if his submission was freely self-chosen and temporally limited, as Philippians 2:4–11 indicates, but this is not what Durst is arguing. He claims the Son's submission is only "functional,"[90] following other complementarians, but he insists again, like other complementarians, that the Son's submission is *eternal* and *person-defining*. This must mean it *is* ontological. The Son's eternal submissive status defines who he *is* in distinction to the Father. To opt for the word "submissive," as I have already argued, is not significant. If Jesus Christ is the eternally submissive Son and cannot be otherwise then he is the eternally subordinate Son; he *is* subordinated God.

Paradoxically, Durst accuses egalitarian evangelicals of arguing that "Triune relationships are an emancipation charter for humanity and a mandate for egalitarian relationships between men and women," and he mentions me by name.[91] This assertion is perverse. I say again, informed evangelical egalitarians do *not* ground the equality of women in triune relationships and do *not* make the Trinity a charter of emancipation.[92] I personally have rejected this argument time and time again. The grounding of the subordination of women in triune relationships is Durst's agenda and it is a distinctively complementarian argument.

He is also mistaken in accusing me of being "a social trinitarian."[93] I am not. A social trinitarian holds that each divine person has his own will. I seek to uphold the creedal and confessional doctrine of the Trinity in which the three divine persons are the one God. A God who is one does not have multiple wills. Again the reverse is the truth. It is Durst and his complementarian friends who either explicitly teach or imply that each divine person has his own will. They believe that the Father's will necessarily triumphs over the Son's will, and so the Son is eternally the submissive or subordinate Son who must obey his father. This understanding of divine relations is undeniably a social doctrine of the Trinity.

In chapter 1 of his book Durst gives a cursory overview of modern discussions of the Trinity which highlights the diversity of opinion current

---

89. Ibid., 300. Here it should be noted that all orthodox theologians believe that the Son is "subordinate" and thus "submissive" in his incarnate state (Phil 2:4–11).

90. Ibid., 300–301.

91. Ibid., 43.

92. I give the evidence for this assertion in my introduction.

93. Ibid., 43.

today in the theological arena, where we find Catholics, Eastern Orthodox, liberals, and evangelicals of various sorts expressing very different views on the Trinity. For me, this is a call to return to the creedal and confessional basis of the doctrine of the Trinity as the criterion on which to evaluate these alternatives, but Durst does not advocate this and we see why in chapter 4. In this chapter he gives an overview of what he calls, "the development of Christian dogma" or the development of "the karma of dogma."[94] He then explains what he means. He says, "**dogma** has to do with historical victories of the orthodox expressions of the faith, **karma**, as used here, has to do with being a victim of orthodox theology and vocabulary." Then he adds, "thank God for the Reformation recovery of *sola scriptura*."[95] This incredibly negative view of the theological tradition is mind boggling. His overview of the historical development of the doctrine of the Trinity then follows in which he introduces the key players and the key terms. In conclusion, he says with these "names, words, and concepts in mind, we are ready to dive back into the New Testament."[96] For the next 150 pages virtually no reference is made to the doctrinal tradition. The implication is that all we need to know about the Trinity is *fully* revealed in Scripture. Thus, without the creeds and confessions of the church as a corrective, he quite openly argues that the Bible teaches "the eternal submission of the Son."[97] This teaching cannot be reconciled with the Nicene faith. As a professor of historical theology he should know this.

The next book published, in April 2016, was Malcolm B. Yarnell's *God the Trinity: Biblical Portraits.* On the back cover, after a list of commendations of the book by some of the best known evangelical theologians, we are told that he is Professor of Systematic Theology at Southwestern Baptist Theological Seminary in Fort Worth, Texas. Yarnell, like Durst, makes his primary focus the Scriptures, and drawing on both the Old and New Testament he establishes some important truths. Chapter 4 is particularly good. He commends contemporary evangelical exegesis and he argues that in doing theology the church fathers have much to teach us. I agree. As an appendix at the end of his book, he gives a modern translation of the three historic creeds, but in the body of the book the creeds and confessions are largely ignored. This is, of course, the great weakness of the book. It is not

94. Ibid., 123.
95. Ibid., 124. The bold is given by Durst.
96. Ibid., 149.
97. Ibid., 300.

informed by the doctrinal tradition and indeed what he concludes stands in contradiction to the doctrinal tradition. Thus, we note that he condemns Calvin and Warfield for limiting the Son's subordination to the divine economy,[98] which is in fact pristine Nicene orthodoxy. For him, the Son is *eternally* "subordinate" to the Father. To deny this (as he rightly notes I have done), he says, leads to "the radical equalization of [the divine persons] of the Trinity in [contemporary] evangelicalism."[99] In reply, I ask, does not the Athanasian Creed speak of the divine three as "co-equal" persons?[100] I have no idea what "radical equalization" may mean. I certainly do not deny God-given male-female differentiation, indicated primarily by our differing bodies, and I certainly do not deny that the Father, the Son, and the Holy Spirit are immutably and eternally differentiated—and I know of no evangelical egalitarian that does in either case. To prove his point that the Son is not subordinate *only* in the economy, he appeals not to the Bible but to Rahner's Rule.[101] His discussion of this "rule" in chapter 6 is hopelessly confused.[102] He notes that there has been much criticism of Rahner's Rule and much debate as to what it indicates, but he is so committed to the complementarian premise that the subordination of the Son in the economy (history) is to be read back into the immanent Trinity that he concludes this is what Rahner is teaching.[103] The possibility that Rahner is saying no more than just as God is triune in the economy so he is in eternity and vice versa, is not even recognized. For Yarnell, the dispute among evangelicals over the Trinity is entirely between evangelical egalitarians bent on furthering their "radical equalization" agenda and complementarians that represent historic orthodoxy![104] He gives no hint at any point in his 2016 book that *some* complementarians may have another view of the Trinity than his own hierarchically ordered one.

Finally, I come to Michael J. Ovey's book, *Your Will be Done: Exploring Eternal Subordination, Divine Monarchy, and Divine Humility* that came out in May 2016. On the back cover he is introduced as the Principal of Oak

---

98. Yarnell, *God the Trinity*, 147.

99. Ibid.

100. Ibid., 151. See also, 152, 217.

101. Ibid, 148.

102. Ibid, 159–77.

103. On page 173 he speaks of "relational differences," which in plain speech means the Father eternally rules; the Son obeys.

104. Ibid., 147, 171–74.

Hill [Anglican] Theological College, London. He is the best known and most outspoken complementarian in England. Like his chapter in *One God in Three Persons*, which I have already mentioned, his book is from cover to cover a defence of hierarchical ordering in divine life. Sadly he passed away in January 2017.

Ovey argues that complementarian trinitarian doctrine represents a "non-Nicene" position[105] that is neither pro-Nicene nor Arian, and as such is to be accepted as an expression of orthodoxy. This doctrine of the Trinity presupposes both the full divinity of the Son (he is "God from God"), and his eternal subordination in authority (he must obey the Father). He appeals to a number of creeds that appeared after AD 340 that teach just this. The problem for him is that the most informed patristic scholars conclude these creeds express *Homoian* Arianism. If this is the case then what Ovey has proved is that the contemporary complementarian doctrine of the Trinity reflects almost exactly Arianism as it was expressed in the middle of the fourth century. The most troubling thing about this book is that Ovey, as an ordained Anglican minister who has given his assent to the three historic creeds and the Thirty-Nine Articles, the Anglican Reformed confession, appeals primarily to *Homoian* Arian creeds of the fourth century, one of which Hilary of Poitiers and Athanasius brand as blasphemous,[106] for his doctrine of the Trinity, rather than the creeds and confessions of the church to which he belongs and is a leader. His ground for this rejection of the faith of the church is that he thinks the New Testament, especially John's Gospel, "teaches 'the Father's primacy of will,'"[107] the Son's eternal "filial obedience,"[108] and specifically, "the eternal subordination of the Son."[109] In other words, he believes that what he thinks as an individual theologian the Bible teaches trumps what the creeds and confessions of the church rule is the teaching of the Bible.

I have been very critical of these four books as one reading them with a pair of creedal and confessional "glasses" on. From my viewpoint, most of what they say on the Trinity is ill-informed or erroneous and contrary

---

105. Ovey, *Your Will be Done*, 34, 2, 3, 12, 37, etc.

106. In support for what I have said, see my discussion of Ovey's argument given in my extended review of Ware and Starke's book, "Extended Review of *One God*."

107. Ovey, *Your Will Be Done*, 77.

108. Ibid.

109. Ibid., 115, 157, 140.

to what the creeds and confessions rule is the teaching of Scripture on this doctrine.

In contrast, for those with unclouded complementarian "glasses" on, these four books represent the triumph of the "orthodox" doctrine of a hierarchically ordered Trinity and the vanquishing of the opposition forces of "evangelical feminism." They prove conclusively that the complementarian doctrine of the Trinity is "what the Bible teaches." On 1 June 2016 I am sure the leaders of the complementarian movement felt elated and superbly confident that the complementarian doctrine of the Trinity had won in the intramural evangelical debate over the Trinity. Their side was united and well-armed and no threats to their supremacy were on the horizon.

Wayne Grudem and Bruce Ware, the *de facto* leaders of the complementarian movement, were so confident that *their* doctrine of the Trinity had prevailed that they made sure that the theme of the 2016 Evangelical Theological Society Annual Conference would be the Trinity. This conference is the largest and most important gathering of evangelicals each year. Participants come from many countries. On average over 2,500 evangelical theologians, most of whom hold a PhD, attend. At the November 2016 conference 2,641 were present. Here I need to point out that in the last ten to twenty years the Evangelical Theological Society leadership and the Conference organizers have been almost entirely of complementarian conviction. Before 2015 the issue of the Trinity would never have been allowed as a conference theme. Opposing voices were not wanted. It was only when complementarians thought they had "won" the debate over the Trinity that they wanted it to be the main topic at the 2016 Evangelical Theological Society Annual Conference.

CHAPTER 2

The Fall of the Complementarian Doctrine of the Trinity

Civil war breaks out

On June 3, everything changed. Civil war broke out in the evangelical community. A deep and sharp split among those who call themselves complementarians suddenly and unexpectedly appeared. The contestants were not divided over the gender question, but rather over the Trinity. Two Reformed women, Rachel Miller and Aimee Byrd, of whom I will say more later, had raised concerns about what was being taught on the Trinity by complementarians prior to June 2016, but the battle only really took off when Dr. Liam Goligher, the respected and able senior pastor of the historic Tenth Presbyterian Church in Philadelphia, made a blistering attack on complementarian teaching on the Trinity. In very strong language he accused Dr. Wayne Grudem and Dr. Bruce Ware, the leaders of the complementarian movement, of breaking with orthodoxy, of idolatry, and of departing from biblical Christianity. He posted his denouncement of their teaching on the Alliance of Confessing Evangelicals website, *The Mortification of Spin.* He begins by rejecting their petty brand of gender complementarianism. He says,

> I am an unashamed biblical complementarian. The original use of that word took its cue from the biblical teaching about the differences yet complementarity of human beings made in the image of God while not running away from the challenges of applying biblical exhortations for wives to submit to their own husbands in the Lord or the prohibition on ordination for women in the

church. . . . But this new teaching [on the Trinity] is not limiting itself to that agenda. It now presumes to tell women what they can or cannot say to their husbands, and how many inches longer their hair should be than their husbands! They, like the Pharisees of old, are going beyond Scripture and heaping up burdens to place on believers' backs, and their arguments are slowly descending into farce.

Then he comments on their grounding of the subordination of women in the supposed eternal subordination of the Son. He says,

They are building their case [for the subordination of women] by reinventing the doctrine of God, and are doing so without telling the Christian public what they are up to. What we have is in fact a departure from biblical Christianity as expressed in our creeds and confessions. . . .

This is to move into unorthodoxy. To speculate, suggest, or say, as some do, that there are three minds, three wills, and three powers with the Godhead is to move beyond orthodoxy (into neo-tritheism) and to verge on idolatry (since it posits a different God). *It should certainly exclude such people from holding office in the church of God.* On the other hand, to say, suggest, or speculate that God's life in heaven sets a social agenda for humans is to bring God down to our level.[1]

And he concludes:

The teaching is so wrong at so many levels that we must sound a blast against this insinuation of error into the body of Christ's church. Before we jettison the classical, catholic, orthodox, and Reformed understanding of God as he is we need to carefully weigh what is at stake—our own and our hearers' eternal destiny.[2]

Wow!

1. Goligher, "Is It Okay to Teach Complementarianism." Italics added. Because I have cut and pasted from this blog, readers should read the text in full. For reasons unknown, in this post, Goligher says, "Egalitarians typically describe the Trinitarian [*sic*] as a divine dance." I have never done this and I certainly do not think the dance metaphor explains the doctrine of *perichoresis*. The truth is that the divine dance metaphor is more at home in complementarian trinitarianism. Complementarians are the social trinitarians. Each divine person has his own will. The dance metaphor is developed by Tim Keller, a leading complementarian and founder of the Gospel Coalition. See his book, *The Reasons for God*, final chapter and p. 215. This is a theme he also develops in more than one of his sermons.

2. Byrd, "Reinventing God."

On 7 June, Carl Trueman, Professor of Church History at Westminster Theological Seminary, Philadelphia, joined in. He fully endorsed what his friend, Liam Goligher, had said and named what they were both opposing as a "species of subordinationism," and, "a position seriously out of step with the historic catholic faith and a likely staging post to Arianism."[3]

A week later, on 14 June, he added,

> Complementarianism as currently constructed would seem to be now in crisis. But this is a crisis of its own making—the direct result of the incorrect historical and theological arguments upon which the foremost advocates of the movement have chosen to build their case and which cannot actually bear the weight being placed upon them. . . .[4]
>
> All Liam Goligher and I did was pull on a rope. The next thing we knew, the whole ceiling came crashing down around us. If that tells you anything at all, it is surely something about how well the [complementarian] ceiling was constructed in the first place.[5]

Bruce Ware[6] and Wayne Grudem[7] both made spirited replies and then the evangelical blogosphere exploded. More than 150 posts were put up on this topic in five weeks. Malcolm Yarnell, the theology department chair at Southwestern Theological seminary, said, "I have never seen anything like it."[8]

All this was totally unexpected and mind boggling. On 16 June 2016, Caleb Lindgren, in an online edition of *Christianity Today*, gave an account of this conflict under the heading, "Gender and the Trinity: From Proxy War to Civil War."[9] At this point the whole evangelical world came to know of the deep and bitter conflict within complementarianism. What Lindgren writes is very stark. He says that some of the best known confessional Reformed theologians have branded the complementarian doctrine of the Trinity "heresy."

What all this clearly makes plain is that the painful and sharp divide among evangelical theologians over the doctrine of the Trinity that had

3. Trueman, "Fahrenheit 381."
4. Ibid.
5. Trueman, "Motivated by Feminism?"
6. Ware, "God the Son—At Once Eternally God."
7. Grudem, "Whose Position Is Really New?"
8. Quote from Lindgren, "From Proxy War to Civil War."
9. Ibid.

been at the back of the stove for about twenty years cannot be simplistically explained as a divide between complementarians and evangelical egalitarians, as most complementarians insisted until June 2016. The divide is in fact between Christians who believe the creeds and confessions of the church express the collective mind of the church and thus authoritatively rule on both what is to be believed and how Scripture is to be rightly interpreted on the great doctrines, and Christians who believe that with Bible in hand they can formulate doctrines individually. Carl Trueman names the groups involved specifically; he says the sharp divide on the Trinity is between the "new Calvinists,"[10] sometimes called New-Reformed, represented by two allied groups, The Gospel Coalition and The Council of Biblical Manhood and Womanhood, and confessional Reformed Christians who consider "Nicene orthodoxy to be a non-negotiable part" of their faith.[11]

Soon after this civil war began, patristics professors Michel Barnes[12] and Lewis Ayres,[13] two of the most respected authorities on the Nicene Faith, were asked where they stood in this debate. In reply, both spoke very disparagingly of the trinitarian theology of Grudem and Ware. On Grudem, Ayres says, what he teaches "about eternal generation is just plain daft." On Ware, he says, his "theology is just a bit too simplistic." He is completely unaware "how deeply and unhelpfully intertwined" is his teaching on the subordination of the Son and the subordination of women. On reading their comments Michael Bird, lecturer in Theology at Ridley Theological College, Melbourne wrote on his blog,

> When two of the biggest names in fourth-century trinitarian theology graciously dismantle your theological argument for basing human relationships on a subordinationist trinitarianism, the game is over. Time to abandon the SS Subordinationism, man the life boats, look for a nice Nicene Island for refuge to land on, and find less complicated ways of arguing for complementarianism.[14]

I think Bird sums up the situation well. Grudem and Ware in particular and all the complementarians who follow them need to raise a white flag and surrender. Their teaching on the Trinity has been judged by their

10. On this movement, see Oliphint, "John Pipers Twelve Features of the New Calvinism;" "New Calvinism," *Wikipedia*, and, Williams, "The New Calvinists."

11. Trueman, "Fahrenheit 381."

12. Bird, "Patristic Scholar Michel R. Barnes."

13. Bird, "Patristic Scholar Lewis Ayres."

14. Ibid.

peers as a blatant denial of the creeds and confessions; a rejection of what the church has agreed is the teaching of Scripture on the one God who is the Father, the Son, and the Holy Spirit, three "co-equal" divine persons.

The contribution of two confessional Reformed women complementarians

In telling the story of how civil war broke out among complementarians over the Trinity in June 2016, the contribution of two brave and theologically-able women must be mentioned: Rachel Miller and Aimee Byrd. They led the way, speaking out before any male theologian broke complementarian ranks.[15] Both stand in the confessional Reformed tradition. Both believe men should lead churches, but they have little sympathy with the way so many complementarians speak of women, and both are convinced that the Grudem-Ware hierarchical doctrine of the Trinity is excluded by the creeds and confessions of the church. Each of them writes with great clarity and theological competence. Aimee Byrd, along with Carl Trueman and Todd Pruitt, host the website *The Alliance of Confessing Evangelicals, The Mortification of Spin*. She writes under the name, "Housewife Theologian." Rachel Miller, on her part, is the news editor for *The Aquila Report* and hosts a website called *A Daughter of the Reformation*.

I think it is true to say that Rachel Miller fired the first shots that led to the civil war among complementarians that began in earnest in June 2016. In 2012 she first raised questions about the way in which many of her fellow complementarians spoke about women.[16] Aimee Byrd followed in her steps, making similar points on the website *The Mortification of Spin*. In February 2013 she wrote a number of blogs critical of patriarchal-complementarianism.[17] She even called this teaching "sanctified testosterone."[18] This criticism of complementarianism was incendiary. For complementarians as a general rule, what they teach they believe is "what the Bible

15. Other complementarian women spoke up after them, some uncritically, supporting Grudem and Ware. See on this, Shellnutt, "The Complementarian Women," and Reissig, "Why Complementarian Men."

16. Miller, "What's Wrong with Biblical Patriarchy?"

17. Byrd, "The UFC and Femininity;" Byrd, "Another Look at the Bikini Question," Byrd, "John Piper's Advice to Women in the Workplace," Byrd, "The Spin of Patriarchy," Byrd, "What Denny Burk Could Do," and Byrd, "Sanctified Testosterone?" Byrd tells me she took the term "testosterone" from a complementarian work.

18. Miller, "What's Wrong with Biblical Patriarchy?"

teaches." Thus, any criticism of their position is a denial by definition of biblical authority and evidence that one is an "evangelical-feminist" and liberal. No matter what strident complementarians may say on women, and sometimes this can be very demeaning, the leaders of the complementarian movement seldom if ever dissent. Fortunately, Byrd had powerful male friends who agreed with her: Carl Trueman and Todd Pruitt. First, in 2013, on the *Mortification of Spin* they asked whether some complementarian teaching could encourage marital abuse,[19] a very threatening question to ask in complementarian circles. And then, clearly in support of what Aimee Byrd had written, Carl Trueman came out with several posts criticizing popular complementarian teaching.[20] I should also mention Andrew Wilson, an English complementarian, who in response to these blogs asked when does complementarianism teaching "slide into sheer silliness."[21]

It is not at all surprising that having begun to criticize the views of some leading complementarians on women, their appeal to a hierarchically ordered Trinity would come under criticism next. Rachel Miller again led the way. In September 2014 she first questioned this teaching[22] and then in May 2015[23] she posted a very critical review of the book *True Woman 101: Divine Design*,[24] conjointly written by Mary Kassian, the Distinguished Professor of Women's Studies at the Southern Baptist Theological Seminary, Kentucky and Nancy Leigh DeMoss, a much published author and radio broadcaster, both complementarians. Miller was forcibly struck by the fact that Kassian and DeMoss grounded the subordination of women in a hierarchically ordered Trinity. As "a daughter of the Reformation" she knew that such teaching contradicted the Nicene Creed. Her post was put up over a year before Liam Goligher and Carl Trueman spoke up in opposition to the Grudem-Ware doctrine of the Trinity. What Miller wrote prepared the way for these men to speak. Aimee Byrd widely publicized Miller's post on the Trinity. These two women then encouraged their male theological friends to stand up on this matter. As a consequence, in June 2016, first

---

19. Trueman and Pruitt, "What the Church Can Do."

20. Trueman, "An Accidental Feminist."

21. Wilson, "When Complementarianism 'Slides into Sheer Silliness.'"

22. Miller, "Is Complementarian Just Another Name for Patriarchy?"

23. Miller, "True Woman 101;" Miller, "Continuing Down This Path Complementarians Lose," and, Miller, "Does the Son Eternally Submit to the Father?"

24. Kassian and DeMoss, *True Woman* 101.

Liam Goligher[25] and then Carl Trueman[26] wrote the posts on *The Mortification of Spin*, noted earlier, openly opposing the Grudem-Ware doctrine of the Trinity. When Rachel Miller saw Goligher's post she "assumed that it would be overlooked, as when she, Byrd, and others had critiqued eternal subordination before."[27] She and Byrd were surprised by what followed. Byrd says, "I invited a man to write [in opposition to the complementarian doctrine of the eternal subordination of the Son] and suddenly, men were concerned and noticed it."[28]

Historians writing on evangelicals in the first half of the twenty-first century, and in particular on the defeat of the error of subordinationism endemic in the complementarian movement at this time, hopefully will not ignore the contribution of these two women. They were the first complementarians to speak out openly against dangerous aspects of complementarian teaching and the male critics followed.

Dr. Robert Letham once more

In telling this story of the rise and rise of the complementarian doctrine of a hierarchically ordered Trinity I discussed the important contribution of Dr. Robert Letham. I pointed out his teaching on "the submission of the Son eternally,"[29] and of the idea that "the Son submits to the Father in eternity,"[30] and his sharp criticism of my work on the Trinity was taken by most complementarians as his legitimation and affirmation of their construal of the Trinity and the complete rejection of mine. They said, if the learned Dr. Letham agrees that the Son is *eternally submissive* and *obedient to the Father*, we must be expressing orthodoxy correctly in arguing that the divine three persons are ordered hierarchically. In the last chapter I made the point that this is a one-sided and not fully accurate reading of what Letham says in his book, *The Holy Trinity*, but this is how most complementarians have read him.

25. Byrd, "Is It Okay?"
26. Trueman, "Motivated by Feminism?"
27. Quoted in Shellnut "The Complementarian Women."
28. Ibid.
29. Letham, *The Holy Trinity*, 398.
30. Ibid., 495.

In my extended review of his book in the *Evangelical Quarterly*[31] I took him to task on these matters and from that time we have been in ongoing friendly dialogue.[32] He is a formidable yet very gracious debating opponent. I think it is true to say that both of us in these exchanges have learnt from the other. In 2012, he wrote the foreword to my book, *The Eternal Generation of the Son*.[33] As far as I am concerned, at this point of time, I cannot single out one issue on the Trinity where I would dissent from his teaching.[34] I was thus surprised to find he had a chapter in Ware and Starke's 2015 book, *One God in Three Persons*.[35] On reading his chapter in this book my concerns were allayed. Letham disagrees with all the other contributors to this book in what he says on the Trinity.

Rightly, he endorses the Nicene doctrines of the eternal generation of the Son and of "inseparable operations."[36] Because the three divine persons work inseparably, he says, "to talk of the 'roles' that each of the persons undertake is potentially misleading."[37] And rightly, like the pro-Nicene fathers, he insists that "Father and the Son are one in being, equal in power and glory, possessing all God's attributes."[38] Again like them, he differentiates the three divine persons on the basis of differing relations of origin. The Father eternally begets and in history sends the Son, the Son is eternally begotten and in history is sent by the Father, and the Spirit eternally proceeds from the Father and in history is "sent by the Son."[39] This, he says, reflects an "order" or "a general pattern"[40] in divine life and operations that is irreversible and unchanging. It does not speak of hierarchical ordering

---

31. Giles, "Review of *The Holy Trinity*."

32. Both in email exchanges and in print. See, for example, Letham and Giles, "An Egalitarian-Complementarian Debate: Is the Son Eternally Submissive to the Father?"; and Giles, "The Evangelical Theological Society," and Letham's reply, "Reply to Kevin Giles."

33. Giles, *Eternal Generation*, 7–9.

34. I speak for myself. Dr. Letham may be of another opinion. For him, the traditional ordering of the sexes remains of huge importance and he is still drawing this into his work on the Trinity in 2015. See his chapter in *One God in Three Persons*, 124–25. So far he has not been able to separate these two matters.

35. Ibid., 109–26.

36. Letham, "Eternal Generation in the Church Fathers," *One God*, 123.

37. Ibid., 123.

38. Ibid., 123 and similarly 122.

39. Ibid., 120–21.

40. Ibid., 121.

in divine life. He says "it is an order of equals, in the identity of the indivisible Trinity."[41] Most importantly, he opposes the primary complementarian argument that the terms "father" and "son" when used of the divine persons are to be understood as human beings understand them. He roundly condemns Drs. Grudem and Ware for making this argument, an argument he says exactly reflects how fourth-century Arians argued and one he judges to be "heretical." He says,

> *The Arian argument* that human sons are subordinate to their fathers led to their contention that the son is subordinate to the Father. The church rejected this conclusion as *heretical* and opposed the premise as mistaken. Rather, the Son is equal with the Father in status, power, and glory. He is identical in being from eternity. In short, to take the creaturely reality as definitive of the life of God is a serious error, leading to dire results.[42]

In my comments on Letham's chapter in my extended review of *One God*, I conclude,

> Compared to what I say in this review in criticism of *One God in Three Persons*, what Letham says is far more telling. It inflicts a mortal blow to the complementarian hierarchically ordered doctrine of the Trinity. He gives a profound and informed rejection of virtually every assertion that the other contributors make and of the primary thesis of this book, namely that the creaturely terms "father" and "son" define the triune relationships of the Creator. He brands this argument for the Son's eternal subordination "Arian," "heretical" and a "serious error."[43]

Dr Letham is certainly now on "the side of the angels."[44] He is opposed to the complementarian doctrine of the Trinity of Grudem and Ware, yet he continues to hold very firmly to what used to be called the "traditional" view of the male-female relationship.

41. Ibid., 121.

42. Ibid., 122. Italics added.

43. Giles, "An Extended Review of *One God in Three Persons*," 26. I sent Dr. Letham my review.

44. I emailed the three sections in this book where I interact with Dr. Letham to him, asking for his critical response. On this comment, he said, "I was under the impression that I was always on the side of the angels! I am not aware that my position has radically changed. I am aware increasingly that the terminology I have used is inadequate and that it is very difficult indeed to search for language that can express what I want to say—an occupational hazard on this topic. The problem is that it can very easily be misconstrued."

The battle at the ETS conference
San Antonio, November 2016

The 2016 ETS conference, as I have mentioned in chapter 1, was planned as a winner for complementarian trinitarian theology. When the call for papers to be given at the conference went out in April, things were looking good for complementarians. They felt they had "won." I put in two proposals for papers on the Trinity. In June I was notified both proposals had been rejected. I was not surprised. Evangelical egalitarians get a very hard time in the Evangelical Theological Society.[45] Two weeks later, Dr. Sam Storms, the incoming president of ETS, wrote to me inviting me to give the opening address in a plenary forum on the Trinity on the first day of the conference, in which Millard Erickson would with me take the "egalitarian evangelical" position on the Trinity and Wayne Grudem and Bruce Ware, "the complementarian position." Few emails I have received over the years have surprised me more. It would be fascinating to know what went on in the halls of power within the ETS at this time. I wrote back accepting this totally unexpected invitation, but pointed out that there was no "evangelical egalitarian" doctrine of the Trinity. I would not speak on that topic. I would, however, be willing to speak on *the creedal and confessional doctrine of the Trinity*. Dr. Storms graciously conceded to my request. I also asked, could someone not allied in any way with the gender debate be invited onto the panel. I suggested by name several confessional Reformed theologians, recommending most warmly Robert Letham. I also raised the possibility of inviting the erudite Catholic theologian Paul Molnar, who was well versed on the debate over the Trinity by evangelicals. This request was denied.

The plenary forum on the Trinity was located in the Ballroom of the Grand Hyatt Hotel. Several hundred theologians, the vast majority with a PhD, were present.[46] I spoke first and spoke bluntly. Mark Woods, the managing editor of the English website *Christian Today*, who was present,

---

45. In 2013 my proposal to give a paper on the eternal generation of the Son at the ETS annual conference was rejected despite the fact that I had just published a book on this topic. A forum on this topic was organized, but I was excluded. I have had five articles rejected by the editor of the *Journal of the Evangelical Theological Society*, all subsequently accepted by international scholarly journals. I could tell similar stories about other egalitarians.

46. For an account of this gathering see, Woods, "Grudem has changed his mind." For my lecture and Dr Erickson's lecture see Giles, "The Nicene and Reformed Doctrine of the Trinity," *Priscilla Papers*, 31.3, (2017), 3–7, and Erickson, "Language, Logic, and Trinity," ibid, 8–15.

wrote, Kevin Giles "was polite but devastating" in what he said.[47] I first pointed out that the Trinity did not set a social agenda; it was our distinctive Christian doctrine of God. No appeal to the Trinity should be made by evangelical egalitarians *or* complementarians for their views for or against the subordination of women. The two doctrines should be considered independently and kept apart. I then pointed out that the Nicene Creed made seven wonderful affirmations about Jesus Christ, the Son of God. In each case, I argued, Dr. Grudem and Dr. Ware explicitly or implicitly denied each one of them. I suggested their most serious error was that they defined the Father-Son relationship in terms of human analogies rather than Scripture. Looking at human life they noted that sons are subordinated to their fathers and by analogy argued that the Son is subordinate to the Father and must obey him. I said that if they turned to Scripture first—which, as professed evangelicals, they should—they would find that in the Bible the title Son, when used of Jesus Christ, speaks of his divine rule as the messianic king, not his subordinate status. One of the seven creedal affirmations I noted, that Grudem and Ware explicitly rejected, was the confession, "We believe . . . the only Son of God [is] *eternally begotten of the Father.*" In other words, both of them denied the doctrine of the eternal generation of the Son, a doctrine on which is predicated everything following that this creed says about the Son.

After I had spoken, Dr. Storms invited Bruce Ware to speak. Dr. Ware began by saying that he and Dr. Grudem now accepted the doctrine of eternal generation. They now thought that the Greek word *monogenēs* used by John and found in the Nicene Creed, which they previously had taken to mean "unique" or "only" (Son), actually means "only begotten" and thus there is a biblical basis for speaking of the Son as "eternally begotten." It was as if the air had been drawn out of the room. After opposing the doctrine of the eternal generation of the Son for at least twenty years, claiming it had no biblical warrant, and convincing large numbers of evangelicals to jettison this doctrine, now they were saying they had been wrong.

Grudem and Ware had rejected this doctrine, they said, because it had no biblical basis, by which they meant, no one text could be found that spoke explicitly of the eternal begetting of the Son. Their "conversion" back to orthodoxy occurred, they explained, when they discovered that *monogenēs* should be translated into English as "only begotten." This then meant that there were texts in the Bible that spoke of the begetting of the

47. Ibid.

Son. Their reasoning behind their change of mind is unconvincing for a number of reasons. To start with, the Greek word *monogenēs* in the five occurrences in which it is found in Johannine writings (John 1:14, 18, 3:16, 18, and 1 John 4:9) almost certainly means "only," in the sense of unique, one of a kind, not "only begotten." The scholarly consensus on this is so strong that it is hard to conceive of it being overthrown.[48] Then there is the problem that the Greek church fathers do not appeal to the word *monogenēs* or any of the texts in which it is found as the basis for their doctrine of the eternal generation.[49] How best to translate *monogenēs* in the fourth-century Greek fathers is debatable because they consistently argue that what makes the Son *monogenēs*/unique is that he alone is eternally begotten. When it comes to the translation into English of *monogenēs* in the Nicene Creed (of 381), confessed by all the churches, the ecumenical consensus is that it should be translated, "only." "We believe in one Lord Jesus Christ, the only (*monogenēs*) Son of God, eternally begotten (*gennaō*) . . . ." And finally, it is to be noted that even if the word *monogenēs* in the Johannine writings meant "only begotten," this is not a basis for a doctrine of *the eternal* generation of the Son.

Notwithstanding these comments, I was pleased to hear both Dr. Grudem and Dr. Ware say that they could now accept what the Nicene Creed says on the eternal begetting of the Son, but what we have to recognize is that their acceptance of this doctrine is irreconcilable with what is basic to their doctrine of the Trinity, namely that what primarily differentiates the Father and the Son is differing authority; the Father commands, the Son obeys. Dr. Grudem says, "Authority and submission between the Father and the Son . . . and the Holy Spirit, *is the fundamental difference* between the persons of the Trinity."[50] If we did not have "subordination [in the Godhead] then there is no inherent difference in the way the three divine persons relate to one another, and consequently we do not have three distinct persons."[51] And again, "If we did not have such differences *in authority* in

---

48. Danker, *A Greek-English Lexicon*, 658; Keener, *The Gospel of John*, 412–15, and Peppard, "Adopted and Begotten Sons of God."

49. Lee Irons sought to support Grudem and Ware's claim that the church fathers based their doctrine of the eternal generation of the Son on the word *monogenēs* that they and he claim means, "only begotten." He invited me to respond to his arguments, which I did. I was able to show his arguments were weak at best and at worst simply wrong. See Irons, "*Monogenēs* in the Church Fathers."

50. Grudem (ed.), *Biblical Foundations*, 31. Italics added.

51. Grudem, *Evangelical Feminism*, 433.

the relationships among the members of the Trinity, then we would not know of any differences at all."[52]

The argument that differing authority is what primarily differentiates persons, human or divine, cannot be defended. I can tell the difference between any two people without knowing what authority one or the other may have. And differing authority certainly does not distinguish men and women; some women have more authority than most men. And when it comes to the divine persons, has not the Son "all authority" (Matt 28:19) and are not the three divine persons all confessed rightly as "The Lord," the supreme ruler? The Nicene faith certainly does not differentiate the divine persons on this precarious basis. In Nicene orthodoxy, what primarily and essentially differentiates the Father and the Son is that the Father is *unbegotten* God, and the Son *begotten* God. Differing *origination* is what distinguishes the Father and the Son.

However, Nicene orthodoxy not only makes the fact that the Father begets and the Son is begotten the one essential difference between them, it also insists that the Father and the Son are both Lord, omnipotent God, and that they are *one in being* (*homoousios*). This word indicates that not only do the Father and the Son *share* the one divine being, but also—and more importantly—that they *are* the one divine being. They cannot be separated in any way, definitely not into a God who rules and a God who obeys. Hierarchical ordering in divine life is inimical to the Nicene faith.[53]

I think at the ETS conference in November 2016 everyone present realized that Dr. Grudem and Dr. Ware had met their Waterloo. The case for a hierarchical Trinity where the three divine persons are eternally differentiated by their differing authority has to be rejected by all who claim to be orthodox Christians. Reporting on this seminar, and specifically on my contribution, Mark Woods, the managing editor of the English news site *Christian Today*, says,

> Giles's lecture is a masterclass in Trinitarian theology. It also represents a determined push-back, in a highly significant evangelical forum, against what is increasingly being seen as an alarming departure from historic Christian teaching by evangelical scholars who are instrumental in forming the theological outlook of new generations of pastors and teachers. Grudem and Ware have

52. Ibid., 433. Italics added.

53. Lindblad, "Stefan Linblad replies," sees exactly the same irreconcilable tension in Ware's current position. See Linblad, "Stefan Linblad Replies."

grounded their complementarian view of men and women on a radical revision of the doctrine of the Trinity. On the evidence presented by Giles, it doesn't work.[54]

Abandonment

The list of confessional Reformed theologians that identify as gender complementarians who have now openly stated that they strongly oppose any suggestion that the Trinity is hierarchically ordered and thus the Son must always obey the Father include the following besides Goligher and Trueman: Aimee Byrd, Todd Pruitt, Michael Horton,[55] Rachel Miller, Stefan Linblad,[56] Scott Swain,[57] Robert Letham,[58] Donald Macleod,[59] Andrew Wilson,[60] and Mark Jones,[61] and this list is certainly not exhaustive. Earlier a few other confessional Reformed theologians of gender complementarian convictions had also bravely spoken in opposition to this teaching: Douglas Kelly,[62] Keith E. Johnson,[63] James J. Cassidy,[64] and Cornelius Plantinga,[65] but they were very careful not to make any criticisms of complementarianism as such. I think it would be true to say that in 2017 there would be very few confessional Reformed theologians who would now support the complementarian doctrine of the Trinity. In addition, we may add to this list those who as far as I know have never publicly come out in opposition to gender complementarianism who probably do not see themselves as confessional-Reformed; Tom McCall,[66] Matthew Emmerson, Luke

---

54. Woods, "Grudem Has Changed His Mind."

55. Horton, "The Eternal Generation of the Son."

56. In a personal email dated 14 August 2016.

57. Swain, "God from God, Light from Light."

58. Letham, "Eternal Generation" in Ware and Stark, *One God*, 109–26.

59. Macleod, "Subordinationism."

60. Wilson, "Complementarianism in Crisis."

61. Jones, "Eternal Subordination of Wills? Nein."

62. Kelly, *Systematic Theology*, 529–62.

63. Johnson, "Augustine's Trinitarian Reading of John 5," and, Johnson, "Trinitarian Agency and the Eternal Subordination of the Son."

64. Cassidy, "Kevin Giles: *The Eternal Generation of the Son*."

65. See Plantinga's introduction to my, *Jesus and the Father*.

66. McCall, "Gender and the Trinity Once More."

Stamps,[67] and Fred Sanders.[68] Finally, I list evangelical egalitarians (some are confessional Reformed).[69] These theologians who were the first (even if many were slow to come to this conviction) to recognize that hierarchically ordering the divine persons was unquestionably a denial of the creeds and confessions of the church: Gilbert Bilezikian,[70] Roger Nicole,[71] Millard Erickson,[72] Philip Cary,[73] Stanley Grenz,[74] Dennis Jowers,[75] Linda Belleville,[76] John Jefferson Davis,[77] Stanley Gundry,[78] John L. Thompson,[79] Graham Cole,[80] Mary Stewart van Leeuwen,[81] Stephen Holmes,[82] Scott McKnight,[83] Ben Witherington,[84] Marianne Meye Thompson,[85] Roger Olson,[86] Mike Bird,[87] D. Glen Butner,[88] Wesley Hill,[89] and myself—and this

---

67. Emmerson and Stamps, "Responding to Bruce Ware."

68. Sanders, *The Triune God,* and in personal conversation.

69. For example, Roger Nicole, John L. Thompson, Mary Stewart van Leeuwen, and Kevin Giles.

70. Bilezikian, *Community* 101, 187–202.

71. See Nicole's comments on the back cover of my book, *The Trinity and Subordinationism,* 2002.

72. Erickson, *Who's Tampering with the Trinity?*

73. Cary, "The New Evangelical Subordinationism," 1–12.

74. Grenz, *The Social God and the Relational Self.*

75. Jowers, "The Inconceivability." 375–410.

76. Belleville, "Son Christology," 59–79.

77. Davis, "Trinity, Gender and the Ordination of Women," 4–7.

78. Gundry, "An Evangelical Statement on the Trinity," 12–13.

79. In personal conversation.

80. Cole, "Trinity without Tiers."

81. Van Leeuwen, *Sword Between the Sexes.*

82. Holmes, "Stephen Holmes's Rejoinder," 154.

83. McKnight, "The Battle Rumbles Along."

84. Witherington, "The Eternal Subordination of Christ and Women." Witherington, "Kevin Giles on the Trinity."

85. Thompson, *The God of the Gospel of John,* and in personal conversation.

86. Olson, "Thoughts about Another Evangelical Controversy."

87. Bird, "Even More on the Complementarian Calvinism Debate on the Trinity." Bird was a late convert. He had written previously in opposition to my account of the Nicene faith and in support of the eternal subordination of the Son. See Bird and Shillaker, "Subordination in the Trinity."

88. Butner, "Eternal Functional Subordination."

89. Hill, *Paul and the Trinity.*

is only a representative list of informed evangelical egalitarian theologians of this opinion. Added together, this is a very significant number of well-respected theologians who adamantly oppose the Grudem-Ware hierarchical doctrine of the Trinity.

It seems that today there are very few evangelical or Reformed supporters of the complementarian hierarchically ordered doctrine of the Trinity. Even the leaders of the complementarian movement now will not endorse the Knight-Grudem-Ware doctrine of the Trinity. Powerful complementarians who a year ago were enthusiastically teaching the complementarian doctrine of a hierarchical ordered Trinity and confidently grounding women's subordination in divine life are now saying they reject this teaching. Al Mohler, the president of the Southern Baptist Seminary, is a very good example. He has done an about-face. Three weeks after Grudem and Ware's teaching on the Trinity was designated heretical by a large number of Reformed theologians, he said, "I do not share their [Grudem and Ware's] proposals concerning the eternal submission of the Son."[90] Similarly, J. Ligon Duncan, the Chancellor of the Reformed Theological Seminary, one time president and now a board member of the Council for Biblical Manhood and Womanhood, who likewise until very recently confidently grounded women's subordination in a hierarchically ordered Trinity, has retreated from this idea. In an almost hour-long lecture, "The Doctrine of the Trinity and Complementarians," given in Houston on 12 November 2016, he sharply draws back from grounding the permanent subordination of women in a supposed eternal subordination of the Son. He says he now contrasts what he calls "pro-Nicene orthodoxy," which he endorses, and the "unique view" of a hierarchically ordered Trinity taught by Grudem and Ware, which he says, the "classical Protestant confessions do not affirm."[91]

In this lecture he tells of the heated and extended debates that went on in June 2016 within the Council of Biblical Manhood and Womanhood. In the end, he says, the council made the decision that the complementarian position does not demand belief in a hierarchically ordered Trinity. In other words, the council agreed that the case for permanent subordination does not necessarily involve belief in a supposed eternal subordination of the Son.

90. Mohler, "Humility and Heresy." Jones, "The Irony of Mohler's Post on the Trinity."

91. My references are from the audio of the talk by Duncan, "The Doctrine of the Trinity and Complementarianism in Recent Discussion."

Following this decision by the Council for Biblical Manhood and Womanhood, the president at the time, Owen Strachan, resigned. For him, like his father-in-law Bruce Ware, and his friend and mentor Wayne Grudem, the Trinity argument is foundational to the complementarian position.

When Owen Strachan resigned, and it was obvious that the complementarian ship was floundering, the board of Council for Biblical Manhood and Womanhood turned to Denny Burk, inviting him to be president, and he accepted. Denny had for years been a fervent supporter of a hierarchically ordered Trinity and of the argument that women's subordination is grounded in the life of God.[92]

After becoming president he too abandoned Grudem and Ware's doctrine of a hierarchically ordered Trinity. He says that, confronted by the pervasive rejection of the complementarian doctrine of the Trinity,

> [I have] done more reading on Nicene Trinitarianism in the last two months than I have ever done previously. It has been good for me, and I am thankful for God for it. . . . [T]he controversy has been unpleasant, but I would not trade the growth that's come from it for anything in the world.[93]

He says, "I now believe in the whole Nicene package," and he openly acknowledges that the complementarian doctrine of the Trinity cannot be reconciled with it. For this reason, he says, he therefore does not agree with "the specific formulations of Grudem and Ware," "my friends." Because he is now personally committed to the Nicene doctrine of the Trinity that excludes hierarchical ordering in the Trinity, he says, "I think it is good and right to leave behind the language of 'subordination.'"[94]

He also says, it has now become clear to me that to be a complementarian who believes in the subordination of women in terms of the Danvers

---

92. See Burk, "Why the Trinity Must Inform Our Views on Gender." He says, we should "not diminish the fact that the analogy between gender roles and Trinity derives not from mere speculation, but from the Bible. The central text in this regard is 1 Cor 11:3. *But I want you to understand that Christ is the head of every man, and the man is the head of a woman, and God is the head of Christ.* . . . First Corinthians 11:3 explicitly links the *masculine-feminine dynamic to the Father-Son dynamic.* The apostle Paul himself invokes the analogy, and our challenge is to understand it and receive it. It's a debate worth having precisely because the link between intratrinitarian relations and gender relations is *transparently biblical.*"

93. Ibid.

94. Ibid.

Statement you do not have to be "reliant upon an analogy" between women and the Son.[95] This comment should be carefully noted. Burk reiterates what Ligon Duncan said. The post-June 2016 position of the Council for Biblical Manhood and Womanhood is that you do not have to believe in a hierarchically ordered Trinity, you can hold to Nicene orthodoxy, which excludes hierarchical ordering in the immanent Trinity, and still be a complementarian. This is a complete about-face by Denny Burk.

"Separating what God has joined together."

In the previous chapter, I documented the consistent claim by leading complementarians—Knight, Grudem, Ware, Burk, Claunch—that the connecting of the subordination of the Son and the subordination of women is "biblical." On this basis, the complementarian consensus has been that the hierarchical ordering of the divine three persons is the basis for the hierarchical ordering of the sexes because this is what Scripture teaches, and 1 Corinthians 11:3 is quoted as proof. Denny Burk, writing in 2013, expressed the then complementarian position unambiguously and strongly. He says,

> [the] analogy between gender roles and Trinity derives not from mere speculation, but from the Bible. The central text in this regard is 1 Corinthians 11:3:
>
> *But I want you to understand that Christ is the head of every man, and the man is the head of a woman, and God is the head of Christ.*
>
> . . . First Corinthians 11:3 explicitly links the *masculine-feminine dynamic to the Father-Son dynamic.* The apostle Paul himself invokes the analogy, and our challenge is to understand it and receive it. It's a debate worth having precisely because the link between intratrinitarian relations and gender relations is transparently biblical.[96]

To say now that we complementarians do *not* believe that the Bible grounds women's subordination in the subordination of the Son is to say that what we have been dogmatically asserting for years as what the Bible teaches was, in fact, mistaken. In other words, we have claimed biblical support for what the Bible does not teach.

95. Ibid.
96. Burk, "Why the Trinity Must Inform Our Views on Gender."

This startling development opens the door to a dialogue with egalitarian evangelicals, who have all along argued that 1 Corinthians 11:3 neither eternally subordinates the Son nor permanently subordinates women. They have argued that in this verse Paul does not order the Father, the Son, and women hierarchically; rather he speaks of three pairs that in each case have one party as *kephalē*. In this specific debate over the interpretation of 1 Corinthians 11:3 we have a classic example of where the Trinity question and the woman question cannot be separated. How 1 Corinthians 11:3 is understood bears on both matters.

What the word *kephalē* means in this text is crucial. This is why it has been so hotly contested. For complementarians to make their "biblical" argument for hierarchical ordering in divine life and for this as prescriptive for the hierarchical ordering of the sexes, the Greek word *kephalē* in 1 Corinthians 11:3 has to mean "head over," or, "authority over." Grudem made a huge effort to prove *kephalē*, when used metaphorically, always has this meaning, but despite all his work he lost the argument.[97] It is now agreed by both complementarians and egalitarians that *kephalē* can have the metaphorical meaning of either "source" or "authority over"[98] and the factual lexical evidence seems to indicate the meaning "head over"/"authority over"/"leader" is very rare.[99] What this Greek word signifies in 1 Corinthians 11:3 must therefore be determined by what Paul says following, in verses 4 to 16. In other words, the context must indicate the meaning. The meaning "head over"/"authority over" in the light of Paul's overall argument makes no sense. Why would Paul say men have "authority over" women in verse 3 and then immediately following say men and women may lead the church in prophecy and prayer (1 Cor 11:4–5)? For him, prophecy is the most important of the gifts of leadership because it builds up the church (1 Cor 14:1–3), and the prophet is "second," coming in order only after apostle and before the teacher (1 Cor 12:28). The meaning "source" or "origin" makes far more sense. This meaning is well attested outside the New Testament, found in Colossians 2:19 and Ephesians 4:15–16, and implied in this passage when Paul, alluding to Genesis 2, speaks of woman coming "from man" (1 Cor 11:8, 12).

Given the case that *kephalē* is best rendered "source" in 1 Corinthians 11:3, we may conclude Paul is making a play on the word *kephalē* using this

97. See Grudem, "Appendix 1: The Meaning of *Kephalē*."

98. Claunch, "God is the Head," 69–72, openly admits this.

99. See Payne, *Man and Woman, One In Christ*, 113–39.

word in a metaphorical sense before speaking of what men and women should have or not have on their literal *kephalē*/head while leading in church assemblies. He says, Christ the co-creator, is the source of humankind, Adam the source of Eve, and God the Father the source of God the Son, in either his eternal generation or temporally in his incarnation.

Since complementarians have now agreed that 1 Corinthians 11:3 does not ground the subordination of women in divine life they may well be thankful that egalitarians have worked out a better way to interpret this passage that does not compel them to conclude that the divine persons are ordered hierarchically and thus breach the Nicene faith.

Why did civil war among complementarians break out in June 2016?

The question I now want to ask is, why did civil war break out among complementarians suddenly and unexpectedly in June 2016? Why did some complementarians come to the conviction that what the leaders of the complementarian movement had been teaching, claiming it was what the Bible taught, all of a sudden become "heresy"?

I believe this civil war had been in the making for some years. My many publications in opposition to the complementarian doctrine of the Trinity were widely known, even if widely dismissed because I was deemed to be one of those dangerous "egalitarian feminists"—as Wayne Grudem consistently designated me. In support of my claim that my writings on the Trinity were well-known by complementarian theologians is the fact that in most of the books on the Trinity written by complementarians, which I discussed in the first section of this essay, I am quoted far more often than any other theologian.

Two widely publicized forums on the Trinity some years prior to 2016 certainly made the evangelical world aware that not everyone was of one mind on the Trinity, but these two events seemed to have had little impact. On 9 October 2008, Trinity Evangelical Divinity School, Deerfield, Illinois, had a public debate in the Seminary Chapel between Wayne Grudem and Bruce Ware on one side and Tom McCall and Keith Yandell on the other side. A big crowd was present.[100] The topic was, "Do relations of authority and submission exist eternally among the persons of the Godhead?" Ware

---

100. Numerous accounts of this debate can be found on the web. I recommend the online *Christianity Today* account by Hanson, "Anathemas All Around."

and Grudem argued in the affirmative, claiming that the Bible taught the eternal subordination and obedience of the Son to the Father and that this was orthodoxy. Yandell and McCall argued in opposition. They said this was not historical orthodoxy and that to eternally subordinate the Son in function, meaning authority, necessarily implied the ontological subordination of the Son. I have been told by people who were present at the debate that they felt more uncertain of what to believe after the debate than before. It was confusing to have theologians taking diametrically opposed positions both claiming the Bible supported their position and both claiming their opponents had fallen into heresy.[101]

In September 2013, the Southern Baptist Seminary in Louisville, Kentucky, had a similar event, but this time it was advertised as an open discussion, not a debate. Bruce Ware arranged the conference and chaired the day. The other participants were Wayne Grudem, Bruce Ware, Fred Sanders, Robert Letham, and Lewis Ayres.[102] Grudem and Ware put the case clearly for the eternal subordination (Grudem) or submission (Ware) of the Son, claiming this is what he Bible teaches and this is historic orthodoxy. Sanders and Letham, who are well-informed trinitarian theologians, put papers, but neither of them took as their agenda to disagree with Grudem and Ware's teaching on the Trinity. Both of them hold similar views to Grudem and Ware on the male-female relationship, and both of them up to this time had not openly opposed the complementarian doctrine of the Trinity, even if both of them had reservations about how Ware and Grudem worded their case.[103] Lewis Ayres gave a scholarly exposition of John 5:19, a much contested text in the fourth-century trinitarian debates. After he had spoken he left to return to England for a wedding. He thus did not take part in the open discussion at the end of the conference. In this hour-long exchange some disagreements on detail were expressed, but neither Letham nor Sanders gave any hints that they rejected hierarchical ordering in divine life or grounding the subordination of women in triune life and relations. Grudem and Ware thought the day confirmed their confidence that what they taught was what the Bible taught and that it was another triumph for complementarians.

---

101. Ibid.

102. I thank Robert Letham for giving me an account of what happened on the day. Another account is given by Sanders, "A Plain Account of the Trinity and Gender."

103. Both of them have told me this.

Next I need to mention a collection of essays, *The New Evangelical Subordinationism: Perspectives on the Equality of God the Father and God the Son*, edited by Dennis W. Jowers and Wayne House, published in early 2012, which I am sure also played a part in what led to this civil war, although in my opinion this part was relatively small. The essays were totally predictable and left the debate as confused as ever. The well-known and articulate complementarians, Bruce Ware, Denny Burk, H. Wayne House, Wayne Grudem, and J. Scott Horrell put the case for a hierarchically ordered Trinity, claiming this was historic orthodoxy and that it prescribed the male-female relationship. Putting the opposing case were those who could be identified as gender egalitarians, Philip Cary, Linda Belleville, David Spencer, Kevin Giles, and Dennis Jowers, none of whom appealed to the Trinity in support of their view that the Bible made the substantial equality of the differentiated sexes, the creation-given ideal. Then to really confuse the debate an article with some additions, much quoted by complementarians, written by a gender egalitarian, Craig S. Keener, was reprinted as a chapter in this book. In this chapter, Keener argues that many texts in the New Testament, especially in John's Gospel, speak of the subordination of the Son and thus to teach the subordination of the Son cannot be heretical. Keener acknowledges that he and I differ on whether or not the subordination of the Son mentioned in John's Gospel and elsewhere is limited to the Son's incarnation or is eternal, but for most readers of this book, this admission would not have clarified matters. Not one gender complementarian could be found by the editors who questioned or rejected the eternal subordination of the Son. The book led nowhere and was largely ignored.

I consider my 2012 book, *The Eternal Generation of the Son: Maintaining Orthodoxy in Trinitarian Theology*,[104] by far the more influential in bringing about this civil war. This book has had a far greater impact on evangelicals than anything else I have written. My previous writings on the Trinity, were widely known, but mostly ignored or dismissed summarily by complementarians. It was very different with my book on the eternal generation of the Son. This was seen by serious theologians as an important contribution to the renaissance of trinitarian thinking by evangelicals. No book had been written on this doctrine for two hundred years, and a defence of the doctrine of the eternal generation was needed because many evangelicals since the Second World War had rejected this creedal

---

104. Giles, *The Eternal Generation of the Son.*

and confessional doctrine. My book has sold very well.[105] In July 2016, InterVarsity wrote to tell me they were doing a second printing and in February 2017, a third printing. The book has been very positively reviewed by Catholics, mainline Protestants, and most of all by confessional Reformed theologians. No author could ask for more affirmation of his work by his reviewers.[106] For the very first time, Reformed theologians who were gender complementarians agreed with me and openly dissented with Wayne Grudem, Bruce Ware, and other evangelicals who rejected the doctrine of the eternal generation of the Son.

I had convinced them that this somewhat esoteric and little understood doctrine of the eternal generation of the Son is foundational to the orthodox doctrine of the Trinity. It guaranteed the two essentials of the trinitarian faith, the full divinity of the Son and his distinction from the Father. To reject this doctrine is to reject the Nicene faith, most authoritatively spelled out in the Nicene Creed. In observing that Wayne Grudem and Bruce Ware both rejected this doctrine, claiming it had no biblical warrant, I pointed out that what they had done was deny the Nicene premise that the eternal generation of the Son is the primary basis for differentiating the Father and the Son. For them, in contrast, the differing authority of the Father and the Son is what primarily and eternally differentiates them. Almost all my Reformed reviewers at this point recognized that the Grudem-Ware doctrine of the Trinity was a blatant denial of the Nicene Faith and the Reformed confessions.

No review caught the attention of the confessional Reformed community more than that by Michael S. Horton, the J. Gresham Machen Professor of Theology and Apologetics at Westminster Seminary, San Diego. I believe it was his review of my book, published in December 2014 in *Modern Reformation*,[107] that made it possible for other confessional Reformed theologians to openly dissent from the Grudem-Ware doctrine of the Trinity. Horton agrees with me; he says to argue that "the Nicene and Athanasian creeds, along with the Anglican Thirty-Nine Articles and the Westminster Confession of Faith, actually teach the eternal subordination of the Son is

105. It is now in its third printing.

106. See O'Reilly, *Reviews in Religion and Theology*; Dallaville, *Theological Studies*; Thompson, *Augustinian Studies*; East, *Restoration Quarterly*; Applegate and Horrell, *Bibliotheca*; Stamps, *Journal of the Evangelical Theological Society*; Olson, "Thoughts about Another Evangelical Controversy"; Cassidy "Kevin Giles: *The Eternal Generation of the Son*"; and Horton, "The Eternal Generation of the Son."

107. Horton, Review of *The-Eternal Generation of the Son*.

profoundly perverse,"[108]and that to teach *the eternal* subordination of the Son "amounts to ontological subordinationism."[109] Most surprisingly, Horton singles out for special criticism, John Frame, the doyen of Reformed theologians, for questioning the eternal generation of the Son and endorsing the eternal subordination of the Son.

Why did it take so long for a civil war over the Trinity to begin?

I must admit that the question that never goes away for me is, why did it take so long for well-informed evangelical and Reformed theologians to come out and say that what complementarians were teaching on the Trinity directly contradicts the teaching of the creeds and confessions of the church? Evangelical theologians who wrote books on the Trinity should have known that to order the persons of the Trinity hierarchically is the essence of the error called "subordinationism."[110] However, almost all the authors of evangelical books written on the Trinity in the thirty years prior to June 2016 said not one word to make their readers aware of this.[111] Their silence individually and collectively is deafening. Robert Letham is one ambiguous exception. As I outlined above, in his 2004 book, *The Holy Trinity*, he accepts that the hierarchical ordering of the divine persons is heresy, and yet when he comes to speak of the male-female relationship he gives lip service to this error. The one unambiguous exception is Millard Erickson. He recognized as early as 1995, in his book *God in Three Persons*, that to speak of the eternal subordination in function or role of the Son implied ontological subordinationism, the primary Arian error. He wrote, "A temporal, functional subordination without inferiority of essence [being] seems possible, but not an eternal subordination."[112]

---

108. Ibid.

109. Ibid.

110. See Giles, "Defining the Error Called Subordinationism."

111. The following are completely silent on this issue. McGrath, *Understanding the Trinity*; Olson and Hall, *The Trinity*; Coppedge, *The God Who is Triune*; George (ed.), *God the Holy Trinity*; Karkkainen, *The Trinity: Global Perspectives*; Leupp, *The Renewal of Trinitarian Theology*; Trier and Lauber, *Trinitarian Theology for the Church*; Fairbairn, *Life in the Trinity*; Holmes, *The Holy Trinity*, and most recently, Sanders, *The Triune God*.

112. Erickson, *God in Three Persons*, 309.

Possible or confessed reasons why most evangelical theologians accepted this hierarchical doctrine of the Trinity or remained silent about it

1. I asked Carl Trueman why he only came out in 2016 and he told me, "I only really became aware of this issue about eighteen months ago." I do not question what he says, but I find it amazing that this dangerous teaching on the Trinity that had for more than twenty years dominated evangelical and Reformed circles was unknown by him. Surely many if not most of his students would have owned a copy of Grudem's *Systematic Theology,* and most of them would have been fully conversant, if not supportive of, the complementarian doctrine of the Trinity and of the sexes. Westminster Seminary is well-known as a bastion of complementarianism. I thus dare to say, Trueman should have known *for years* that most evangelicals and Reformed Christians had come to accept that the divine persons were hierarchically ordered in the immanent Trinity.

2. When I asked other complementarians why they had not spoken against the all-too-common claim that the divine persons are ordered hierarchically, I was surprised by how many told me that they said nothing because they thought this was teaching so wrong it was below their dignity to comment on it. They may excuse their silence on this basis, but I say in reply, if you recognized that this teaching was "so wrong" you should have spoken out.

3. Third, as we think of how so few spoke against this teaching we have to recognize that in the evangelical world there is an abysmal ignorance of the doctrine of the Trinity. What this means is that large numbers of evangelical and Reformed people did not realize that to hierarchically order the divine persons is to contradict the faith of the church. I have said publicly many times when speaking to theological graduates and post graduates in Australia and America that in my introductory course on doctrine/theology at my seminary we had many lectures over several weeks on the doctrine of Scripture, many lectures on the atonement, and then all the other doctrines, including the Trinity, were covered in one lecture. And I have added, "we never got back to the Trinity in the next three years of my four year course." In every case those present laughed in agreement. When I began seriously to read on the Trinity in 2000, in a week or so I found that I

knew more about this doctrine than my friends who were lecturers in theology. What this means is that when evangelicals began arguing for hierarchical ordering in the Trinity and quoting texts in support and claiming this was historic orthodoxy they met with virtually no opposition. Evangelical ignorance of the primary doctrine of the faith, our distinctive doctrine of the triune God revealed in history and Scripture, and spelled out carefully in the creeds and confessions of the church, had left wide open the door for error to enter and take over the evangelical house.

4. I now offer a fourth explanation. In the last twenty years I have been invited to speak at numerous seminaries and colleges in the United States, usually by an evangelical egalitarian on the faculty. I think in every case I have been told the same story. My host has said to me, "I am pleased to have you speak because I need to keep my head down. Most of the faculty are complementarians and any criticism of their position on women or the Trinity is not tolerated. For me to openly dissent would cause a painful split among the academic staff. I would be marginalized." They said to me, in other words, that not to dissent avoids conflict and the making of implacable enemies. I suspect this has been a very common reason why most evangelical and Reformed theologians have not protested against this teaching; the cost was too great. I can understand this. We male theologians want the acceptance of our colleagues, especially the great ones of our tribe who have been until very recently predominantly one-eyed complementarians. I personally know the cost of breaking with the evangelical and Reformed tribe. I have been castigated as a "feminist," a "liberal,"[113] and much worse, excluded on principle from publishing in many evangelical journals, and shunned by many evangelicals, especially those who like to call themselves "Reformed."

Here we must recognize that for many complementarians what they believe about women is not just one of many doctrinal beliefs they hold. It is of huge importance for them. Indeed, all too often it seems to be the most important doctrine for them. In their minds it distinguishes true evangelicals from pseudo evangelicals. Why this is so is a fascinating question. I make no attempt to answer it in this book. The huge importance for complementarians to endorse without any criticism the whole complementarian package became very clear

113. See for example, Grudem, *Evangelical Feminism*, 115–18, 259.

to me when a one-time friend and fellow graduate of Moore Theological College in Sydney said to me very angrily, "Kevin, we [complementarians] will never give way to you on the Trinity because to do so would weaken our case for male headship, and nothing is more important for us."

5. There is, however, a fifth reason why virtually no evangelical or Reformed theologian spoke in opposition to the complementarian doctrine of the Trinity before June 2016. Complementarians had convinced themselves that what they taught on women *and* the Trinity is "what the Bible teaches." To disagree was thus by definition to reject biblical authority. What this argument did was shut down completely any critical and independent thinking, the most important academic virtue. People who argued that the Bible in fact does not teach the creation-given subordination of women and/or the eternal subordination of the Son were not to be listened to, no matter what evidence they offered. They were shut out and ignored because in questioning "what the Bible teaches" they had revealed themselves to be "liberals" and "evangelical feminists" who do not accept the authority of Scripture. This certainly silenced any criticism of any aspect of complementarian teaching, except by the foolhardy or the very brave.

Now we see the huge importance of the recent rejection of the complementarian doctrine of the Trinity by complementarian confessional Reformed theologians. They have said, to Grudem and Ware, the leaders of the complementarians, what you have been teaching on the Trinity is *not* "what the Bible teaches," according to the creeds and confessions of the church. You have let your great concern to uphold male "headship" as you understand it corrupt your reading of the Scriptures on the Trinity.

Why the evangelical egalitarians were the first to take up arms

Now we can see why evangelical egalitarians were the first by a long shot to recognize and reject complementarian teaching on the Trinity. They had for years been condemned as "liberals" and "feminists" who rejected the authority of Scripture for arguing that the Bible makes the substantial equality of the two indelibly differentiated sexes the creation-given ideal, the subordination of women being entirely a consequence of the fall (Gen

3:16) and thus not good. Adding criticism of complementarian teaching on the Trinity could not lose them any more friends, or further harm them. They had nothing to fear.

Millard Erickson it seems was the first to recognize that complementarian teaching on the eternal subordination of the Son in authority implied by necessity ontological subordinationism, as I noted above.[114] The first detailed and telling refutation of this teaching was given by Gilbert Bilezikian in his article "Hermeneutical Bungee-Jumping: Subordination in the Godhead," published in the *Journal of the Evangelical Theological Society* in March 1997. He concludes that what Grudem and the early Letham teach "comes dangerously close to Arianism" and he asks that all teaching on the eternal subordination of the Son be rejected as heretical. This is a wonderful pioneering piece of work, very well grounded in Scripture and history. What he argued was either rejected outright or ignored by most evangelicals. Next followed my first work on the Trinity, *The Trinity and Subordinationism*, in 2002, which—as I point out in a subsequent book, *Jesus and the Father: Evangelicals Reinvent the Doctrine of the Trinity* (2006)—met with a blistering attack on me personally and on what I argued.[115] It took several years before large numbers of egalitarian evangelicals came to agree that to teach the eternal subordination of the Son breached historic orthodoxy as defined by the creeds and confessions, but they were far ahead of their complementarian friends in coming to this conclusion.

Where do we go from here on the Trinity?

Caleb Lindgren, the *Christianity Today* journalist who in June 2016 let the evangelical world know that civil war had broken out among complementarians over the Trinity, was present at the ETS plenary forum on the Trinity in San Antonio in November 2016 when Ware and Grudem dropped the bombshell that they now accepted the doctrine of the eternal generation of the Son, and Millard Erickson and I criticized their teaching on the Trinity in front of several hundred evangelical and Reformed theologians. You would certainly think this was newsworthy, but not one word on all this was reported in *Christianity Today*.

114. Erickson, *God in Three Persons*. He concluded on page 309 that, "A temporal, functional subordination without inferiority of essence [being] seems possible, but not an eternal subordination."

115. I tell this story on pages 10 and 11 of my *Jesus and the Father*.

But it is not only *Christianity Today* that has gone silent on this hugely important theological revolution that has taken place within evangelical and Reformed circles. Once the initial explosion of blogs on the Trinity in June and July 2016 were posted very little more appeared. All went quiet. As far as I can see, hardly anything on what has taken place that I have recounted in this book has been mentioned in evangelical publications, especially those controlled by complementarians. It would seem that there is tacit agreement by all involved that *this embarrassing defeat for complementarians is to be swept under the carpet and never mentioned again.*

I for one do not think we can now simply move on as if this civil war had not taken place. Grudem and Ware have been accused by many well-informed and influential Reformed theologians of contradicting the creeds and confessions of the church, and by doing so, of "heresy" and "idolatry."

Carl Trueman, a gender complementarian, names those he thinks are responsible for leading the evangelical world into trinitarian heresy. He places the blame squarely at the feet of "the leaders" of what he calls "the new Calvinists," whose voice he says is expressed by The Gospel Coalition and the Council of Biblical Manhood and Womanhood.[116] Addressing them he says,

> It is thus surely time for somebody of real stature in the New Cal-
> vinist world to break ranks with the Big Eva establishment and
> call out this new subordinationism for what it is: a position seri-
> ously out of step with the historic catholic faith and a likely staging
> post to Arianism. For if this is allowed to continue with official
> sanction or simply through silent inaction, then the current New
> Calvinist leadership will have betrayed the next generation in a
> deep and fundamental way.[117]

On his part, Liam Goligher, another gender complementarian, concludes that to deny "classical Trinitarianism, or Orthodox Christianity . . . should certainly exclude (such) people from holding office in the church of God."[118]

It seems to me, that what is demanded at this point of time is that every evangelical and Reformed theologian should now publicly state where they stand on the doctrine of the Trinity. Large numbers, possibly the majority of evangelicals and Reformed theologians, have agreed that

116. Trueman, "Fahrenheit 381."

117. Ibid.

118. Goligher, "Is It Okay."

to argue that the Son is eternally subordinated or submissive to the Father and must obey him is to break with what the creeds and confessions of the church unambiguously teach. They have conceded that the complementarian doctrine of a hierarchically ordered Trinity is "heresy."

I ask, where do you stand?

Addendum:
The term "heresy"

I and others have accused Wayne Grudem, Bruce Ware, and by implication all complementarian theologians who argue for the eternal subordination of the Son, thus construing the Trinity as a hierarchy, of falling into "heresy" and called their views on this matter "heretical." It is therefore vital that I define how I use this term. The word can mean very different things to different people.

In the New Testament, the Greek word *hairesis* is used descriptively of those of one opinion in distinction to those of another opinion without any necessary pejorative overtones (e.g., Acts 5:17; 15:5; 1 Cor 11:19; Gal 5:20). However, in the second half of the second century, when destructive divisions in the church emerged, the term developed strongly negative overtones. The word began to be used of those who were thought to be undermining the faith of the apostles. The binary opposites soon became orthodoxy and heresy.[119] The next development was to conclude that one needed to hold to orthodoxy to be saved; heresy led to damnation. Alister McGrath argues that in modern times the word "heresy" has taken yet another meaning. In scholarly literature it now "designates teaching that emerges from within the community of faith on the one hand, yet is ultimately destructive of the faith on the other." It is "an intellectually defective vision of the Christian faith."[120]

In my usage, and I hope that of the confessional Reformed theologians who in June 2016 came out in opposition to the teaching of Grudem and Ware on the Trinity, to designate what someone is teaching as "heresy" is not to suggest that the one giving this teaching is outside the Christian faith and thus will not be saved. I believe we are saved by grace through faith in Christ, not on the basis of a theological examination we must pass on the

119. So McGrath, *Heresy*, 36–39.
120. Ibid., 83.

last day. I in no way question Wayne Grudem or Bruce Ware or anyone other complementarians standing as a fellow Christian.

Before I say, how I use this term, I need to reject another meaning often heard in evangelical circles. Many times I have heard "heresy" defined as "the denial of what the Bible teaches." I do not use the word in this sense because the evangelical world is deeply divided on many of the most important doctrines and we are divided because we cannot agree on what the Bible teaches on these doctrines. Evangelicals are of opposing opinions on grace, the meaning and scope of the atonement, the return of Christ, the doctrine of the church, church government, baptism, women in leadership, and much more. I definitely do not think that whatever conclusion we have reached on any of these matters we should judge fellow evangelicals who are of another opinion guilty of "heresy."

For me, the term "heresy" is rightly used to designate teaching that directly denies the ecumenical creeds and the confessions of the church. These documents represent what the church has agreed is the teaching of Scripture, invariably after painful and protracted debate and division. These written and public statements of doctrine reflect the *consensus fidelium*, the consensus of the faithful, rather than the private opinion of individuals. This today is the most common understanding of the word, "heresy." This is how many dictionaries define the word. For example, the *Concise Oxford Dictionary* gives the meaning, an, "Opinion contrary to the orthodox doctrine of the Christian church."[121]

Dr. Ware and Dr. Grudem and anyone else are free to break with the *consensus fidelium* and in doing so express their personal opinion, their *hairesis* in the biblical meaning of this word, but they need to honestly admit what they are teaching is not the faith of the church. It is their opinion.

Finally, I return to McGrath's definition of heresy. It "designates teaching that emerges from within the community of faith on the one hand yet is ultimately destructive of the faith on the other." It is "an intellectually defective vision of the Christian faith."[122] I think this definition perfectly captures the complementarian doctrine of the Trinity. It has emerged within the evangelical and Reformed community of faith and yet it has been

---

121. *Concise Oxford Dictionary,* 1964, 572. Similarly, the Merriam-Webster dictionary gives the primary meaning of the word as, "a religious opinion contrary to church dogma." https://merriam-webster.com/dictionay/heresy. "Dogma" is not a negative term for Reformed and Catholic theologians. It speaks simply of what the church has agreed is to be believed.

122. Ibid., 83.

destructive of that faith. By explaining and defining divine life and relations in terms of human life and relation complementarians fell into what is possibly the most serious of all theological errors—idolatry; making God in our own image. We evangelicals should not define divine fatherhood and divine sonship by appeal to human experience, as liberal theologians are wont to do. We should define divine fathership and sonship in the light of scriptural revelation.

In the New Testament, Jesus Christ is called the Son/Son of God to speak of his kingly status, not his subordination. As the Reformed theologian and complementarian John Frame says,

> There is a considerable overlap between the concepts of Lord and Son. . . . Both [titles] indicate Jesus' powers and prerogatives as God, especially over God's people: in other words, [the title Son speaks of his] divine control, *authority*, and presence.[123]

---

123. Frame, *The Doctrine of God,* 658. Italics added.

CHAPTER 3

Doing Evangelical Theology

I n chapter 1, I outlined how the complementarian doctrine of the Trinity
came to the ascendancy in the evangelical and Reformed world in recent years. A number of well-known and much published evangelical
theologians were able to get millions of believers to accept a hierarchical
doctrine of the Trinity, a doctrine excluded by the creeds and confessions
of the church, and to reject the doctrine of the eternal generation of the
Son, a doctrine enshrined in the Nicene and Athanasian creeds and in the
Reformation and post-Reformation confessions of faith. They were able
to do this because they claimed that their teaching was "what the Bible
teaches" and because they made their hierarchical doctrine of the Trinity
the primary theological basis for the subordination of women—something
of huge importance to many evangelical and Reformed men and women.
Thus, to question their hierarchical doctrine of the Trinity necessarily was
to question their hierarchical ordering of the sexes. It seemed that inextricably connecting these two things fused many a theological brain.

Then suddenly and unexpectedly, as I outlined in chapter 2, the
whole deck of cards came tumbling down. This teaching on the Trinity
that seemed to have won the day was denounced as heretical and idola-
trous by well-known and respected confessional Reformed theologians,
and soon after abandoned by many of the most well-known and respected
complementarians.

In this chapter I am going to argue that the complementarian theologians got the doctrine of the Trinity wrong because they had a wrong
understanding of how evangelical theology is "done."[1] They thought that

---

1. Parts of this chapter reflect wording and ideas from chapter 2 of *The Eternal Generation of the Son* by Kevin Giles. Copyright (c) 2012 by Kevin Giles. Used by permission
of InterVarsity Press, P.O. Box 1400, Downers Grove, IL 60515, USA. www.ivpress.com.

with Bible in hand they were free to construct the doctrine of the Trinity with virtually no reference to the historical development of this doctrine or any reference to the creeds or confessions of the church. In their mind systematic theology was simply a summary by individual theologians of what they thought the Bible teaches on any doctrine. For them, an evangelical who believed in the inerrancy of Scripture had in the Bible the answer to every theological question.

The Bible alone is the basis for doing theology

We find a classic expression of the view that to "do" theology all we need is the Bible in Wayne Grudem's *Systematic Theology*, possibly the most influential systematics text in evangelical and Reformed circles in the last twenty years. He subtitles his work as *Biblical Doctrine*. We see why when he comes to define systematic theology. He says "it is any study that answers the question, 'What does the Bible teach us today about any given topic.'"[2] In this definition there is no mention of the contribution of "tradition" or "reason," two technical terms that I will explain below, that orthodox theologians insist also make vital contributions to the theological enterprise. Because, for Grudem, the Bible gives the content of the great doctrines, he excludes on principle the idea that doctrines develop and take shape in history, and that there can be objective advances on what is said explicitly in Scripture in the "doing" of theology.

Grudem says he works with just two presuppositions:

(1) that the Bible is true and that it is, in fact, our only absolute standard of truth;

(2) that the God who is spoken of in the Bible exists, and he is who the Bible says he is: the creator of heaven and earth and all things in them.[3]

The possibility that other presuppositions may impinge on his interpretation and systematizing of Scripture and on his theological conclusions is not seen as a possibility. The implication is that if you affirm that the Bible is inerrant you will be able to give inerrant accounts of any doctrine by appeal to the Bible *alone*. Our fallen nature will be saved from itself.

2. Grudem, *Systematic Theology*, 21.

3. Ibid., 26.

I quote only Grudem, but this understanding of "doing" theology is endemic in the evangelical world. This is what I was taught at Moore Theological College, Sydney, in the late 1960s. Our theology lecturer, Dr. Broughton Knox, told us in every lecture, "what I am teaching you is what the Bible teaches." These words echoed in my head for twenty years. I used to often say in my sermons, "All I believe comes directly the Bible." Sometimes Dr. Knox would make reference to the Thirty-Nine Articles, the Anglican Reformed confession of faith, in agreement or disagreement, but the Articles were never the subject of lectures. I also see this understanding of theology in almost all the chapters in Ware and Starke's book, *One God in Three Persons,* and in Roderick Durst and Malcolm Yarnell's books on the Trinity. For these theologians, all you need is the Bible to get a right doctrine of the Trinity, or any other doctrine. There is no discussion on what the creeds and confessions teach and no acknowledgement whatsoever that in fact the doctrine of the Trinity was developed in history by theologians with first-class minds in the context of bitter and ongoing debate about God's triunity.

It is this understanding of theology that has undone complementarian theology. Following this methodology, complementarian theologians led the evangelical world into heresy on the foundational doctrine of the Christian faith, the Trinity. It is heart-warming for evangelicals to be told that what is being taught comes directly from the Bible and to denigrate creeds and confessions and ignore the contribution of the theologians, but in the end it is disastrous. It results in evangelicals becoming a sect of Christianity with their own distinctive doctrines.

An acerbic evaluation of the claim that "my theology comes directly from Scripture" is given by the great Reformed theologian Abraham Kuyper. He calls such assertions "unscientific," "grotesque," and "utterly objectionable."[4] He says,

> There is, to be sure, a theological illusion abroad . . . which conveys the impressions that, with the Holy Scriptures in hand, one can independently construct theology. . . . [T]his illusion is a denial of the historic and organic character of theology, and for this reason is inwardly untrue. No theologian following the direction of his own compass would ever have found by himself what he now confesses and defends on the ground of Holy Scripture. By far the largest part of his results is adopted by him from theological

4. Kuyper, *Principles of Sacred Theology,* 574.

tradition, and even the proofs he cites from Scripture, at least as a rule, have not been discovered by himself, but have been suggested to him by his predecessors.[5]

In these words, Kuyper asserts in very strong language that theology does not spring directly from the text of Scripture and that no theologian independently constructs theology. Rather, theology historically develops, communally not individualistically, and thus has an "organic" character.

Evangelical theologians may claim that they are getting their doctrine directly from Scripture, but in truth the "theological tradition" in which they stand determines to a large degree what they conclude and claim to be entirely "biblical."

A far better understanding of the theological enterprise

To suggest that systematic theology is nothing more than the systematizing of what Scripture explicitly and obviously says is untenable. Systematic theology draws deeply on exegesis and on biblical theology, but it is a distinct discipline that invariably needs to say things not explicitly said in Scripture.[6] The exegete and biblical theologian have as their charter the task of giving the *historical meaning* of Scripture; what it meant to the writers and hearers; atomistically in the first case, synthetically in the second. Both are *descriptive disciplines*. The more rigorous the biblical scholarship, the more diversity within Scripture is highlighted by both the exegete and the biblical theologian. For example, a critical study of how Paul speaks of the law makes it undeniable that he says different things in different contexts. And when it comes to biblical theology, this too highlights diversity. For example, we are now, thanks to redaction criticism, aware that the theologies of Matthew, Mark, Luke, and John are very different. We must acknowledge that the enthusiastic acceptance of critical scholarly methods by evangelicals in the last forty or more years has forced on us a deeper appreciation of the diversity in Scripture. What this means is to say my theology/doctrine

---

5. Ibid., 574–75.

6. For helpful discussions on the nature of systematic theology from an evangelical perspective, see McGrath, *Genesis of Doctrine*; Stackhouse, *Evangelical Futures*; Lints, *The Fabric of Theology*; Grenz, *Revisioning Evangelical Theology*; Grenz and Franke, *Beyond Foundationalism*; Franke, *The Character of Theology*; Griggs, *New Perspectives for Evangelical Theology*.

comes *directly* from Scripture is a denial of the diversity in Scripture. It implies uniformity not present in Scripture.

Systematic theologians in contrast have as their charter the task of addressing the church in each succeeding generation. Karl Barth expressed this point eloquently when he said, "Dogmatics [by this term he was referring to what English-speaking people generally call systematic theology] does not ask what the apostles and prophets said but what we must say on the basis of the apostles and prophets."[7] Systematic theology is an ongoing *prescriptive discipline.* In the light of Scripture and any other information that may help them, theologians have the responsibility of answering theological and ethical questions, often of a complex nature, that have arisen in their age and culture, long after the closing of the canon. Their job is to tell the church of their day what should be believed and how Christians should behave. Almost invariably the Bible, written long ago in another culture, does not specifically address the contemporary question being asked. In seeking to answer questions on what Christians should believe and how they should behave on any matter arising long after the apostolic age, systematic theologians by necessity not only look to the Bible but also to how other Christians past and present have dealt with this question or a related one, *and* they use their minds. The more deeply they think the more likely they will come up with good answers. I have just mentioned three things that are always part of "doing" theology. They are often called the three "sources" of theology: Scripture, tradition, and reason. I call them "sources" reluctantly because they are not three buckets from which information is drawn in equal amounts, but rather three *contributing elements* in the "doing" of theology. We might even call them, "resources." What is meant by the terms "tradition" and "reason," and how all three "sources" contribute to the theological enterprise needs explaining.

1. Scripture

For most theologians, and emphatically so for evangelical and Reformed theologians, Scripture is the primary "source." Saying this is the easy part. *How* Scripture informs theology is the hard part. I give a number of reasons why this is so.

First, when theologians turn to Scripture they invariably find, as I have just mentioned, that the Bible does not speak with one voice on the issue in

7. Barth, *Dogmatics*, 1.1, 16.

focus. This is where division most often occurs and the worst mistakes are made. It is easy for theologians to find a text or texts that seem to confirm what is important to them. In answer, other theologians with a wider and deeper grasp of Scripture dissent. The great Athanasius was the first to confront this problem and characteristically he gave an answer that has never been bettered. In reply to Arius, who selectively quoted texts to prove what he already believed, Athanasius argued the locus of theology is always the whole "scope" of Scripture.[8] What this meant for him was that individual texts could never be allowed to trump what the whole of Scripture taught. This principle later came to be known as "the analogy of faith."[9] This term has a long history,[10] and it has not always been understood in the same way. But for the Reformers it meant that the exegesis of any one passage could not be right if it contradicted "the faith" as revealed in all of Scripture.

Because of this diversity in scriptural teaching no one verse, or even two, three, or four verses, can ever settle a complex theological question. The whole of Scripture must be the locus of theology. For this reason, texts that are discordant with what all of Scripture would seem to teach must be interpreted in the light of the whole. They cannot be absolutized. The quoting of "clear and unambiguous texts" in order to prove that what is being taught is what the Bible teaches is a perennial problem. Athanasius faced this problem when Arius quoted Proverbs 8:22, "the LORD created me at the beginning of his works," which he took to be referring to the Son of God. The sixteenth-century Reformers faced this problem when the Catholics quoted James 2:24, "A person is justified by works and not by faith alone" (Jas 2:24).

The best discussion that I have ever read of the problem created for theologians by discordant texts in Scripture is by Professor Oscar Cullman in his book *The State in the New Testament*. He wrote in the early 1950s when the question he had to answer as a theologian was, why did so many German Christians support Hitler? His answer is that the Germans in the post-First-World-War period longed for a strong state that would bring

8. Athanasius, "Discourses against the Arians," 3.26.29 (p. 409).

9. The textual support traditionally given for this term, Romans 12:6, is dubious. Here Paul says the prophet should prophesy "in proportion to faith." Faith in this verse would seem to refer to the subjective faith of the prophet, not "the faith" of the community (meaning, for Protestants, what the church has come to believe is the overall teaching of Scripture).

10. For helpful and information discussions of this concept see Blocher, "The Analogy of Faith" and Kaiser, "Hermeneutics and the Theological Task."

honor back to the German people and achieve political stability. When Hitler achieved this they found in one text, Romans 13:1, justification for obeying Hitler no matter what he did. This text supported what they already believed, namely that loyal citizens should give total obedience to the state and its ruler. For Cullmann, writing with the history of the totalitarian Nazi state fresh in his mind and living day by day in the shadow of a totalitarian Communist state, one text—or even two or three texts—taken in isolation could never be the basis for a doctrine of the state, or any other doctrine. He says that if Romans 13:1 is read to sum up all that the Bible teaches on the state then this one verse stands in "flagrant contradiction to the teaching of Jesus. It would also contradict the opinion of the other New Testament authors as well, chiefly that of the author of the Johannine apocalypse. Above all, moreover, Paul would contradict himself."[11] To avoid such a stark contradiction within Scripture, Cullmann argues for an alternative reading of Romans 13:1 that allows it to be harmonized with what is said elsewhere in Scripture on the state. This he does in two ways. First, he places this text in its specific first-century historical context. Paul is endorsing the rule of Rome which *at that time* was promoting peace and stability in the empire and so making possible the advance of the gospel. And second, he places this text in the context of what the Bible as a whole taught on the state, and here he highlights the teaching of Jesus that limits the rule of the state to what is the state's domain (Mark 12:17), and Revelation chapter 13 that teaches that the state can become an instrument of the devil.

Now I move to a second challenge theologians face when they turn to Scripture to find an answer to a complex theological question. Often they often find that the Bible does not say anything explicitly or directly about the pressing theological question they are seeking to answer. In the next chapter, in discussing how the doctrine of the Trinity emerged in history, we see a classic example of this. Possibly the most difficult question the early theologians had to answer was how can God be one and three? The Bible does not directly answer this question. Modern examples of this problem would be abortion or gambling. When the Bible does not specifically speak to a question demanding an answer, theologians have to *infer* what they think the whole of Scripture indicates.

A third challenge theologians face when they turn to Scripture in their age and culture is that they often find that the Bible does not address the question their contemporaries are asking. For modern theologians,

11. Cullman, *The State*, 46.

especially twenty-first-century theologians, this is a huge problem. Western culture and thinking is so different to that of biblical times. An example of this challenge that arose very early is infant baptism. In the first century, probably the only people who were baptized were believers, people who had responded to the gospel, but then in the second century the question became, should the children of believers be baptized, because they cannot be considered pagans? Because the Bible does not address this question baptism has remained a contentious issue. A contemporary example is the debate about the status and ministry of women. The Bible certainly reflects a patriarchal culture where women are subordinated to men. So the apostles exhort women to be subordinate in that cultural and historical context (Eph 5:22; Col 2:18; 1 Pet 3:1). The question that arose in the late twentieth century was, what does the Bible say on the man-woman relationship in a profoundly egalitarian culture?

A fourth challenge theologians face when they turn to Scripture is that they find that doctrines are not given in Scripture as propositions. What the Scriptures say on any doctrine is always contested. Doctrines are the fruit of debate and division over what Scripture says and the outcome of deep thought by the best of theologians. Nowhere is this truer than with the doctrine of the Trinity. Another example is the doctrine of salvation. The sixteenth-century Reformers had to work hard and long to formulate a doctrine of salvation that excluded the idea that the church mediated salvation.

How then is inspired Scripture the primary "source" of theology?

I suggest the following: when faced with a pressing theological question, evangelical and Reformed theologians should go first to Scripture and carefully consider what it says on the matter in focus, listening to everything said from Genesis to Revelation. If, as almost invariably always is the case, no obvious or univocal answer can be found in Scripture, then debate should be welcomed. Two or more minds are always better than one. In listening to those of another opinion the issues become clearer and how the Bible speaks to the question better understood. What I have just said illustrates the fact that "doing" theology is a *communal exercise*. It is in an ongoing and communal listening to Scripture so that gradually the church comes to agree how the Bible points to the right answer to the theological question dividing the church.

Before leaving this discussion on the contribution of Scripture in the theological enterprise I need to say that for the Reformers the Latin catch cry *sola scriptura,* by Scripture alone, did not mean, *solo scripture.*[12] It meant rather that Scripture alone is divine revelation and as such is uniquely authoritative in matters of faith and practice. The claim by modern evangelicals that it meant for them *solo scripture,* "Scripture only," is simply mistaken.

2. Tradition

What is handed down from the past is called "tradition." The sixteenth-century Reformers distinguished between two kinds of church tradition. They may be helpfully designated, "tradition 1," the exegetical and theological tradition, and "tradition 2," teaching authorized by the church that is independent of Scripture.[13] The Reformers highly valued "tradition 1," but for them "tradition 2" had no authority at all. It should be the same for evangelicals today.[14]

"Tradition 1," the exegetical and theological tradition, should be highly valued because it reflects how the best of theologians from the past have understood the Scriptures on issues in dispute. Their conclusions have been codified in the creeds and confessions of the church. These documents do not stand over Scripture or have the same authority as Scripture. Rather, they sum up after a time of conflict and debate what the church has agreed is the teaching of Scripture on the central doctrines of the faith and thus to be believed, *and* they prescribe how Scripture is to be read on these doctrines. If we ignore the weighty guidance of the creeds and confessions, as complementarian theologians have done, we are bound to fall into error.

"Tradition 1" also speaks of the communal nature of systematic theology. Theologians not only need to listen to other theologians of their own

12. See, Vanhoozer, *Drama of Doctrine,* 156 and Award, "Should We Dispense with *Sola Scriptura?*"

13. I adopt the terminology of Heiko Oberman, given in his book, *The Harvest of Medieval Theology,* 371–75.

14. In addition to the books listed earlier on the nature of systematic theology see, Williams, *Retrieving the Tradition and Renewing Evangelicalism;* Williams, *Evangelicals and Tradition;* Williams (ed.), *Tradition, Scripture, and Interpretation;* Hall, *Learning Theology with the Church Fathers;* Vanhoozer, *Drama of Doctrine.*

day, they need also to listen to the great theologians of the past. "Tradition 1" is nothing less than the collective wisdom of the whole Christian community, past and the present. There is, of course, a degree of authority in the tradition from the past. It reflects many hundreds of years of debate and theological reflection. Karl Barth, in one of his profound asides, says, to denigrate or dismiss "the tradition" is to break the fifth commandment, "Honor your father and mother."[15]

This communal wisdom from the past, confessional theologians believe, is the best safeguard we have to avoid the danger of reading our own agenda into the Bible when "doing" theology.[16] The premise is that if we listen carefully to what the creeds and confessions of the church teach we will learn how the church in the past understood the teaching of Scripture on the doctrines articulated in those creeds and confessions. One of the foundational insights provided by the study of hermeneutics in the last thirty years is that everyone comes to the text of Scripture with beliefs and presuppositions that they have inherited. Kevin Vanhoozer says that twentieth-century hermeneutics has shown that "exegesis without tradition—apart from participation in the history of the texts reception—is impossible."[17] The "traditions" we hold can be private and unwritten, and informed by all sorts of influences, some good and some bad, or, in the case of creeds and confessions, public and written down and expressing the agreed mind of the church. I am arguing that the traditions of the latter kind are the surest, the most trusted, and therefore the best beliefs/presuppositions to bring to our theological reading of Scripture.

The great importance the Reformers gave to "tradition 1" is well illustrated in the First Helvetic Confession of Faith of 1536. Article 2 says that "divine scripture is to be interpreted in no other way than out of itself and is to be explained by the rule of faith and love." Article 2 continues, "Where the Holy Fathers and early teachers, who explained and expounded scripture, have not departed from this rule, we want to recognize and consider them not only as expositors of Scripture, but as elect instruments through whom God has spoken and operated."[18]

In contrast, modern evangelicals all too often devalue at best, and dismiss at worst, the creedal and confessional tradition. As we noted earlier

---

15. Barth, *Church Dogmatics*, 1.1, 16.

16. So Trueman, *The Creedal Imperative*.

17. *The Drama of Doctrine*, 113.

18. See Cochrane, *Reformed Confessions*, 100–101.

in this chapter Grudem does not even mention it in his account of what is involved in doing theology. He does, I admit, often appeal to creeds and confessions and to some of the great theologians of the past, but only to assert that they agree with him, which certainly with the Trinity they do not. In his book *Evangelical Feminism: A New Path to Liberalism*,[19] he gives a whole chapter to arguing that I seek to "trump" the authority Scripture by arguing that the creeds and confessions of the church are our best guides to the right interpretation of the Bible on the Trinity or any other doctrine. It is his view that the Bible *alone* should settle doctrinal questions.

Paradoxically, this discounting and denigration of creeds and confessions, so common in evangelicals circles today, with its concomitant belief that the Bible alone is all the Christian needs to "do" theology, finds its origins in late-eighteenth-century American Protestant liberalism, driven by Enlightenment ideals. It was at this time that the slogan first became popular, "no creed but the Bible." The theologians who used this slogan said that they were seeking only get back to the simple beliefs of the first Christians. This sounded like a good move, but the result was a denial of key elements of the Christian faith.[20]

This is what complementarians have done unwittingly by following this path. Claiming that all that is needed to do theology is the Bible, the most significant complementarian theologians have led their brothers and sisters into error. Thy have constructed a doctrine of the Trinity that reflects word for word their theology of the male-female relationship, and have found many texts that seem to support their views, but the outcome has been a denial of what the creeds and confessions teach. This is hugely problematic because for confessional Christians the creeds and confessions are simply what the church across the centuries has agreed is the teaching of the Scriptures.

What has struck me most forcibly in reading this literature, and I have covered most of it, is that the writers make no attempt to listen carefully to the great trinitarian theologians of the past, Athanasius, the Cappadocian fathers, Augustine, Aquinas, Calvin, etc., or to the many fine modern expositions of their teaching, or to the creeds and confessions of the church.[21] True, we often find appeals to these people or to the creeds, claiming that they teach what the modern complementarian author teaches, but they

19. Grudem, *Evangelical Feminism*, chapter 12.

20. See further, Hatch, "Sola Scripture," 62.

21. I make the proviso again that Robert Letham stands apart.

are almost always without a factual basis. None of these great theologians or the creeds endorse what Knight, Grudem, Ware, and those who follow them teach on the Trinity. Rather, they exclude their teaching.

Kyle Claunch, a complementarian, writing in *On God in Three Persons*, edited by Bruce Ware and John Starke, openly admits this. Speaking specifically of the trinitarian teaching of Wayne Grudem and Bruce Ware, he says, their "understanding of the eternal relationship between the Father and the Son," in which the Son must eternally submit his will to the will of the Father, "runs counter to the pro-Nicene tradition, as well as the medieval, Reformation, and post-Reformation Reformed traditions that grew from it."[22]

3. Reason

"Reason" is the most nebulous of the so called "sources" of theology because different theologians have seen it contributing to theology in different ways. Thomas Aquinas held that reason can discover basic theological truths, such as the existence of God, but the higher truths, such as the doctrine of the Trinity, are given by revelation. The Enlightenment thinkers who gave rise to theological "liberalism" went even further. They argued that reason can provide *all* that we need to know about the world, ourselves, and God. In direct opposition to such views, evangelical theology insists that what we know of God and his ways is given by revelation. What we know about God is revealed by God, not discovered by human reason.

Nevertheless, we evangelicals should accept that "reason", enlightened by the Holy Spirit, makes an important contribution to the theological enterprise in many ways. For example, it makes possible the understanding and analysis of what is revealed in the text of Scripture. It is also the facility that makes theology possible. If evangelical theology does not spring directly from Scripture, good minds enlightened by the Spirit of God will be needed to find coherence within the diversity in Scripture and draw appropriate inferences from what is given in Scripture.

In reflecting on the contribution of Christian minds in the theological enterprise we must also recognize that in the very act of systematizing we make a step forward from what is said in individual texts. The great advocate for the inerrancy of the Bible, B. B. Warfield, speaking of the contribution of reason in the formulating of doctrines said, "The mind brings

22. Claunch, "God is the Head of Christ," 88.

to every science something which though included in the facts, is not derived from the facts considered in themselves alone, or as isolated data."[23] In other words, the whole is more than the sum of the parts. Not surprisingly, Warfield goes onto argue that systematic theology is a "progressive science,"[24] which makes "organic growth"[25] through an "historic process."[26] More recent discussions of what is involved in "doing" theology often call this constructive contribution of reason, model- or paradigm-building. In doing so they reflect the use of these terms in science to explain what is involved in theory construction. A model or paradigm in this usage is a way of seeing all the data in a unified way so as to make sense of the parts and in doing so advance scientific understanding.

The constructive and additive contribution of theologians with the best of minds who have listened long and hard to the Scriptures and to how they have been understood in the past should be fully appreciated. Athanasius, as much as anyone, illustrates what one exceptional theologian can give to the progress of theological clarification and theological development. As we will see in the next chapter, many of the most important theological advances in the formulation of the doctrine of the Trinity were made by him.

And to sum up

Let me make crystal clear what I am arguing. I am putting the case that theology, specifically evangelical theology, is always more than just systematizing what is explicitly said in Scripture. Rather, it develops in history, almost always in conflict and debate, and almost always what in Scripture answers the question before the church at any particular time is at first unclear and disputed. Coming to a common mind as to what in Scripture answers the question before the church usually involves giving more weight to some comments in Scripture than others and often demands making *inferences* or *deductions*, on the basis of what is said in Scripture because the Scriptures do not directly address the matter in dispute. In this communal exercise focused on the Scriptures, what the ancient church decided these Scriptures are saying is invaluable to us, and must not be ignored if

23. Warfield, "The Idea of Systematic Theology," 53.

24. Ibid., 75, 76, 79.

25. Ibid., 75.

26. Ibid., 76.

codified in creeds and confessions. In this complex, interactive, and communal enterprise, the theologians with the best minds make the biggest and most important contribution. I am also arguing that in this historical and organic process *objective advances* are made in theological articulation that go beyond anything explicitly said in Scripture, and yet the Christian community comes to agree that what is concluded captures the trajectory that Scripture itself implies.

In the next chapter, I am going to illustrate how what I have spoken about in the abstract and theoretically in this chapter can be seen concretely and practically in play in the formulation and development of the Nicene doctrine of the Trinity.

How the Doctrine of t̶
in History and Wha̶
and Is Now O̶

I n this chapter I illustrate what is involved in "doing" evangelical theology by studying how one doctrine developed in history, the doctrine of the Trinity. And in telling this story I will summarize the key elements in this doctrine as they were established progressively one by one. In outlining how the orthodox doctrine of the Trinity was formulated incrementally in history I make it clear that the claim that "my doctrine of the Trinity comes directly from Scripture" is untenable. It is simply not true. The truth is, as Gregg Allison, an atypical historically informed complementarian, says, "the doctrine of the Trinity was hammered out very early in the church's existence," only "reaching a settled conviction by the end of the fourth century."[1] Making much the same point, Alister McGrath says, "the doctrine of the Trinity is *the end result of a long process of thinking* about the way in which God is sent and active in the world."[2]

Basic to what I say in this chapter is my conviction that we can only properly understand and accurately articulate the orthodox doctrine of the Trinity if we know how it developed in history. This is true of all the great doctrines, but none more so than the Trinity. The pathway to understanding at some depth any doctrine is always the historical pathway. Scripture does not explain why a doctrine emerged, what specific questions it sought

---

1. Allison, *Historical Theology*, 231.

2. McGrath, *Studies in Doctrine*, 198. Italics added.

ed disputes within the church. The history of the
information. I thus agree completely with Khaled
ys, "the [historical] development of trinitarian doctrine
ts meaning,"[3] and Robert Letham who says, "To think clearly
e Trinity, we must grapple with the history of discussion in the
ch."[4] Now we see why so much evangelical work on the Trinity in the
last thirty or so years has been so thin and often a denial of historic orthodoxy. Too many evangelicals have simply made up their doctrine of the
Trinity, picking and choosing texts that seem to support what they want to
believe, without any real depth of understanding of how this hugely important doctrine was hammered out in history and for what reasons. This is
why they have led the church into error.

The story of the development of the orthodox doctrine of the Trinity in history

The New Testament authors certainly believed that God is one God and
three persons, and thus we may say that belief in the triunity of God is
foundational to the Scriptures. However, *the doctrine of the Trinity*, such as
given in the Nicene Creed of 381, is not found in the New Testament. This
developed in history in the context of prolonged and sharp debates as to
what the Bible taught on God's triunity and in the end included a number
of theological conclusions that had no specific textual support, and yet were
endorsed by the church because it was agreed that these conclusions followed the trajectory that Scripture set.[5]

The two great challenges the theologians of the third and fourth centuries AD faced were, first, that the Bible seemed to say contradictory things

3. Anatolios, *Retrieving Nicaea*, xv.

4. Letham, *The Holy Trinity*, 2.

5. The account of the doctrine of the Trinity I give in what follows is the fruit of
fifteen years of reading, writing, lecturing, and debating with complementarian theologians on the Trinity. It reflects closely my article, "The Orthodox Doctrine of the Trinity:
part 1, the Doctrine in Summary; Part 2, Commentary." This article was given by CBE to
the over 2,500 attendees at the 2013 annual Evangelical Theological Society conference.
I invited comment and criticism and got none. Before publication I sent this account
of the doctrine of the Trinity to twelve well-known and published trinitarian scholars,
asking them to critically comment on it and if possible give their endorsement. Several
suggested a few cosmetic changes and nine endorsed the statement. In this list of endors-
ers, I mention Paul Molnar, John Webster, Christopher Hall, Keith E. Johnson, and Neil
Omerod. The others did not want their name listed publicly.

on the Father-Son relationship and, second, that they were called on to answer questions about the Father, the Son, and the Spirit that the Bible did not explicitly answer. Before anything of lasting import could be established these two hurdles had to be jumped. They had first, to quote McGrath, to find a "sophisticated whole" in "the remarkably complex biblical witness"[6] and, second, to draw conclusions—make inferences—that invariably went beyond anything Scripture actually said. The early theologians could not avoid facing these two very difficult challenges because in the fourth century the church became sharply and painfully divided on its understanding of the Father-Son relationship and resolution was demanded. In the debate with Arius and his followers, what made matters so difficult and complex was those on both sides held the same high view of Scripture. The authority of Scripture was not the issue; it was the big-picture, how the Scriptures as a whole were to be understood, that caused all the division and pain.

I now outline how the doctrine of the Trinity developed step by step in history and what was concluded.

1. God is one

The belief that God is one is grounded firmly in Scripture. The first Christians as Jewish believers were agreed that God is one. They knew that to Moses God disclosed his name to be YHWH (Exod 3:14), and that he insisted that he alone is to be worshipped (Exod 20:2–6; cf. Isa 42:8; 44:6; Zech 14:9). The belief that God is one is eloquently affirmed in the so-called *Shema*, the Jewish confession that says, "YHWH our God, YHWH, is one" (Deut 6:5; cf. Isa 45:5). In the New Testament, the belief that God is one continues to be affirmed by Jesus and the apostles (Mark 12:29; Rom 3:30; 1 Cor 8:4–6; Eph 4:6; 1 Tim 2:5; Jas 2:19).

Nevertheless, the earliest Christians, assuming that the one God is the Father, the Son, and the Spirit, interpreted the Old Testament to be foreshadowing what would be revealed in the New Testament. They thus took many Old Testament texts to be speaking prophetically of the Messiah, identified as the Son of God (e.g., Ps 2:7; 2 Sam 7:14), or as Wisdom (Prov 8:22–31). And they applied texts that spoke of YHWH, translated as *Kurios*/Lord, in the Greek Old Testament, directly to Jesus Christ (Acts 2:21; Rom 10:13; 1 Cor 1:31; 10:26; 2 Cor 10:17, etc.). And, they concluded that the Spirit of God spoken of in the Old Testament was to be identified

6. Ibid., 200.

with the Spirit that came on Jesus at his baptism (Mark 1:9–11) and on the first Christians at Pentecost (Acts 2:17–21). What this indicates is that the apostolic writers believed that the Old Testament foreshadowed the triune understanding of God revealed in history by the advent of Jesus Christ and the coming of the Spirit on all believers. On this premise they interpreted the Old Testament.

2. God is three

In the New Testament we find a clear and unambiguous revelation that the one God is three "persons." This revelation first of all takes place in history. One day Jesus of Nazareth began speaking as if he were speaking for God and he did things that only God can do and the Spirit becomes active in a way hitherto unknown. These events demanded explanation and this is given in verbal revelation. At Jesus' baptism, the Spirit of God descended on him and God declares, "You are my Son, the beloved, with you I am well pleased" (Mark 1:11). The first thing this narrative makes clear is there are three actors in this drama, God in heaven, the Spirit who comes down from heaven, and Jesus of Nazareth, who is called God's Son. For Jesus to be named God's "beloved Son" (*agapētos*) indicates that he stands in a family relationship with the one who speaks from heaven. He is the beloved or unique Son of God; the Son of the God Jesus identifies as "my Father." In giving their account of Jesus' ministry, death, and resurrection, the Gospel writers recount how step by step the disciples came to recognize that Jesus is in fact the long-awaited Jewish Messiah (Matt 16:13–16), God visiting his people. After his resurrection, Thomas discloses the disciples' final position. He falls down before Jesus declaring him to be, "My Lord and my God" (John 20:28).

The conclusion that the one God is somehow three "persons" appears again the last verses of Matthew's Gospel where the risen Christ commissions his disciples, "Go therefore and make disciples of all nations, baptizing them in the name [singular] of the Father and of the Son and of the Holy Spirit" (Matt 28:19). This three-fold understanding of God is implicit throughout the New Testament. In more than seventy passages the three divine "persons," Father, Son, and Spirit, are associated together as if they are on an equal footing and alike God.[7] In these triadic verses, the Father

7. For more on this see Giles, *Jesus and the Father*, 109–10 and Durst, *Reordering the Trinity*, 68–82, 309–18.

is named first twenty-nine times (Matt 28:19; Rom 5:1–5; Gal 4:4–6, etc.), the Son is named first twenty-nine times, (Rom 14:17; 1 Cor 6:11; 2 Cor 13:14, etc.) and Spirit first seventeen times (Luke 24:49–50; John 15:26; 1 Cor 13:14, etc.).[8]

The belief of the early Christians that God is "three persons" never led them to abandon their primary belief as Jews that God is one; in monotheism. Nevertheless, in John's Gospel, God is God the Father in distinction to God the Son (John 1:1–14; 1:18; 3:16–17, 31–36). Nowhere in the New Testament is the tension between confessing God as one and the Son as God more clearly expressed than in the opening words of John's Gospel. "In the beginning was the Word [and John identifies Jesus with the Word] and the Word was with God, and the Word was God." The Father and the Son are both God yet two persons, and to further stretch our minds to breaking point, Jesus says, "I and the Father are *one*" (John 10:30; 17:22). We must also note that John speaks of the Son as *monogenes*, (John 1:14, 18; 3:16, 18; 1 John 4:9). This Greek word almost certainly means, "only" in the sense of "unique"; "one of a kind."[9] He is not *a* son of God. He is *the* Son of God, the long-awaited Messianic King; God visiting his people Israel.

Paul definitely continued to affirm monotheism, but his understanding of monotheism included the Father, Son, and Spirit. Nowhere is this expanded monotheism more clearly seen than in 1 Corinthians 8:5–6, where Paul confesses both "one God the Father" and "one Lord Jesus Christ." In these words Paul boldly adapts the wording of the foundational Jewish confession, the *Shema*, given in Deuteronomy 6:4, "The LORD our God is one," to speak of the one God who is both the Father and the Son. In this text, Paul only mentions the Father and the Son, but it is evident from his many triadic comments that the one God is in fact the Father, the Son, and the Spirit (Rom 15:16; 1 Cor 12:4–6; 2 Cor 13:13; Eph 4:2, 18–20; etc.).

In every one of his epistles, Paul begins with a greeting or opening blessing in which God is designated as "our Father" or "the Father" or "the Father of our Lord Jesus Christ." The last of these, "the Father of our Lord Jesus Christ," is particularly common (Rom 1:7; 1 Cor 1:3; 2 Cor 1:2; Gal 1:3, etc.). What this indicates is that the term "Father" is for Paul not simply an equivalent for the term God (*Theos*), but the identification of one divine person, God the Father, who stands in relation and distinction to

---

8. I take these numbers from Durst, *Reordering the Trinity*, 70.

9. Danker, *A Greek-English Lexicon*. 658; Keener, *The Gospel of John*, 412–15; Peppard, "Adopted and Begotten Sons of God," 92–110.

the Son. But these greetings reveal more than this. In each case the blessing is from the Father and the Son coordinately; one source, one God. When Paul identifies Jesus as God's Son, he uses the definite article. Jesus Christ is "*the* Son (of God)." His relationship with the Father is unique. He is not like any human son.

I have spoken above of the divine three as "persons." This word needs comment. The Latin-speaking Tertullian was the first to speak of the Trinity as "*tres personae, una substantia*" ("three persons, one substance"). For him, and other Latin theologians the word *personae* spoke of what is three in God and *substantia* of what is common to all three. The Greek fathers used the word *hypostasis* for what is three in God and *ousia* (being) for what is one in God. The word "person" has its limitations because all creaturely words used of the Creator cannot be taken to mean exactly what they mean when used of creatures. In this case, we must not take the word "person" when used of the divine three to imply three individuals like we would if we were speaking of three people.[10] Nevertheless, the divine three are best called "persons" because they are revealed in history and Scripture as person, as those who love, relate, speak, and act like persons. We have no better human word to describe them.

3. How is the one God three persons?

The very first trinitarian question the post-New Testament theologians had to answer is, how can God be one and three? The Bible does not directly give an answer. In the second and early third centuries a number of inadequate answers were offered. Some argued that God is a solitary monad

---

10. In speaking of God, we must use human words. We have nothing else, and God must use human words to speak to us, if we are to understand him, but human language is *human* language. Words that refer to our created world are inadequate when used of God, who is not a creature: he is eternal and uncreated. All the key trinitarian terms, "father," "son," "person," "relation," "unity," "sending"/"mission," "begotten," and "procession" are thus not to be taken "univocally"—or to use everyday non-technical language, "literally"—when used of God. The content of the creaturely terms used of the divine is ultimately revealed knowledge apprehended by long and prayerful reflection on God's self-revelation to us in Scripture. To give these words content primarily on the basis of human experience results in God being depicted as a human being, which is idolatry. The Arians made this error. They took the names "father" and "son" and the term "begotten" literally, and on this basis argued the divine Son came into being in time and like all human sons he was set under the authority of his father. Human language used of God is best described as "analogical."

who simply reveals himself sequentially in history, first as God the Father, then as God the Son, and finally as God the Holy Spirit.[11] Today we call this understanding of God's threeness, "modalism." This answer was rejected because much in the Bible excludes this understanding of God's triunity. In Scripture, God the Father, God the Son, and God the Holy Spirit are depicted as existing and acting at the same time, and as distinct persons, not just modes or revelations of the one God.

The next inadequate answer to the question of how God can be one and three was given by the Apologists, most notably, Justin Martyr, Irenaeus, and Tertullian. They argued that the Father was God in a unique sense and in history he manifested his Word and his Spirit, who were each God, but in a secondary sense. This is called "economic trinitarianism"—God is only triune in the economy (history), not eternally. This answer did not win the day because in this case the Son and the Spirit are not God in the same sense as the Father, if for no other reason than they are not eternally three distinct "persons." The Apologists wanted to be faithful to what Scripture taught, to affirm a fully triune understanding of God and endorse the full divinity of the Son, and yet how they construed God's triunity resulted in them failing in all of these aims. After Nicea, Warfield, says their doctrine of the Trinity in fact became "heterodoxy."[12] Nevertheless, we must thank God for their theological contribution to the historical development of the doctrine of the Trinity because in all conceptual work, preliminary and inadequate answers must first be given for them to be improved and perfected. In getting a better answer, Allison says, more "sophisticated thinking" was needed.[13]

Arius offered a third solution and found much in Scripture to support his view. He too began with the premise that God the Father is the one God, a monad, arguing that in time he created a Son who was far above all other creatures, but not God in the same sense as the Father. For him, Proverbs 8:22 proved his case. This verse spoke of God creating Wisdom in time, and in the New Testament Wisdom is identified with Jesus Christ (1 Cor 1:30; Col 1:15–20, etc.). He noted that Jesus himself said "the Father is greater than me" (John 14:28), and that the Father sends the Son (John 8:42; 17:3, 23, etc.); the Son does the will of the Father (John 4:34; 5:30, etc.). And he observed that Paul taught that on the last day the Son will hand over

11. See further Giles, *The Eternal Generation*, 96–97.

12. Warfield, "The Idea of Systematic Theology," 78.

13. Allison, *Historical Theology*, 234.

his rule to the Father (1 Cor 15:28). Thus, for Arius, on the basis of what he thought Scripture taught, Jesus Christ, the Son of God, is *subordinate temporally*, he is created in time; *subordinate ontologically*, he is not God in the same sense as the Father; and *subordinate relationally*, as a son he has to obey his father.

In God's good plan, the best and brightest theologians in the early fourth century lived in Alexandria, Arius' home city. Origen recognized, before Arius came on the scene, that if Jesus Christ is God—and he concluded he was—and the Spirit is God, then the Father, the Son, and the Spirit are alike eternal and this means that the God of the Bible is not a god who in time becomes three; the God of biblical revelation is eternally triune. This answer, Alexander Bishop of Alexandria, and his successor Athanasius, one of the greatest theologians of all times, endorsed. From then on every orthodox Christian theologian has agreed: God's oneness and his threefoldness is eternal. The one God is for all eternity the Father, the Son, and the Holy Spirit. Even if God had not created the world or come into the world to save he would be triune. The Scriptures nowhere say this, but once this answer was inferred it became "orthodoxy" because it made sense of all that was revealed in Scripture.

We should also thank God for Arius as we do for the Apologists. What Arius and his followers taught, says Allison, "exerted a great impact on the early church's development of Trinitarian doctrine."[14] Arius forced the best of theologians of his day to think hard and long about how theology is "done." He raised two questions that had to be answered. How is it that Scripture can be quoted profusely to deny what would seem to be primary in Scripture, in this case, the full divinity of Christ and his unqualified Lordship? And, second, are theologians limited to what Scripture explicitly says? Below we will see how the first question was answered, the seemingly contradictory comments in Scripture about Christ. On the second question, the answer was that theologians not only could, but should, make inferences based on what Scripture actually said. It was their duty to follow the trajectories Scripture itself implied. Given these two answers, the bishops at the council of Nicea in 325, were able to articulate a profound doctrine of the Trinity that was both predicated on Scripture and made sense of all of Scripture. Later at the Council of Constantinople in 381, Allison says, the bishops gathered and "reworked the creed of Nicea, . . . [producing a] creed with a clearer affirmation of the deity of both the Son

14. Ibid., 238.

and the Holy Spirit."[15] "Further developments awaited the contribution of Augustine."[16] As is so often the case, says Allison, "fierce controversy"[17] in the church was the path to faithful doctrinal definition.

4. The one God is eternally self-differentiated as the Father, the Son, and the Holy Spirit

Next came the question how is the God who is eternally triune self-differentiated? Again the Bible does not directly answer this question. Building on the observations of the Apologists that the Son's coming forth "from" the Father is described in Scripture as a birth or a begetting, metaphorically speaking, the Greek theologians of Alexandria of the early fourth century developed the doctrine of the eternal generation of the Son.

This doctrine explained how the Son of God is self-differentiated from God the Father and yet not less than the Father in any way. This doctrine was needed because Arius argued that the Son was other than God the Father since he was *created in time.* He is God in second degree. In opposition, Athanasius and later the Cappadocian fathers argued that the Son is *eternally begotten* by the Father and thus of the same being and power as the Father (on the premise that a human son is of the same being/nature as his father).

The theological inference that the Son is to be understood to be eternally begotten of the Father the Pro-Nicene Fathers predicated primarily on the revealed names, Father and Son. A father-son relationship implies a generative act. This deduction was both suggested and confirmed by Scripture. The most important texts pointing to this conclusion were Psalm 2:7, which speaks of a future "begetting" of a royal son, and Proverbs 8:25, which speaks of the "begetting" of divine Wisdom before creation. These texts they understood to be prophetic because in the New Testament they are interpreted christologically. The Greek-speaking church fathers did not appeal to John's use of the word *monogenes,* which they understood to mean "unique," as the basis for the eternal begetting of the Son. However, for them, what made the Son unique more than anything else was that he alone is (eternally) begotten of the Father.[18]

15. Ibid., 241.

16. Ibid.

17. Ibid., 238.

18. For more detail on the doctrine of eternal generation, see Giles, *The Eternal*

One of Augustine's very important theological contributions was his conclusion that the Bible, in speaking of the Son as *"from* the Father," envisages both an eternal *and* a temporal "from the Father." The temporal missions of the Son and the Spirit are antecedently anticipated by the eternal processions of these persons within the Godhead. What this means is that what takes place in eternity within the life of God constitutes the persons, not what takes place in history. The economy simply reveals what is eternally true.[19] Again I make the point; the Bible does not say this. This is a profound theological deduction or inference that once articulated is seen to capture what Scripture implies. Allison commends Augustine for such "unique touches" in the development of the doctrine of the Trinity.[20]

In Nicene orthodoxy, and Augustine certainly reflects this, the doctrine of the eternal generation of the Son is the foundation on which the doctrine of the Trinity rests. It is the linchpin that holds together the two absolutes in the orthodox doctrine of the Trinity, oneness in divine being and the eternal and immutable differentiation of the divine persons. Nevertheless, no text in Scripture can be quoted to teach the eternal generation or begetting of the Son. This doctrine is an inferred doctrine that once formulated is confirmed as "biblical" by the fact that it makes sense of so much in the Bible.

The great importance of the theological conclusion that the Son is eternally begotten of the Father is seen in the central christological clause in the Nicene Creed, the most authoritative account of the trinitarian faith of the church. Here the full equality of the Son is predicated on his eternal begetting by the Father, and this is mentioned twice. The Creed says,

> We believe in one Lord, Jesus Christ, the only (*monogenēs*), Son of God, *eternally begotten of the Father,* God from God, Light from Light, true God from true God, *begotten not made,* of one being (*homoousios*) with the Father.

What these words affirm is that the Son on the basis of his eternal begottenness is as much God as the God the Father and yet he is other than God the Father; he is God the Son. To be "from" the Father, this creed teaches, in no way entails diminution of any kind.

Generation of the Son.

19. Hill, *The Trinity,* 4.5.29 (p. 174). The italics added.

20. Allison, *Historical Theology,* 241.

5. The Father and the Son are *homoousios*

What is common to the three divine *personae* (persons), the Latin-speaking Tertullian said, is *una substantia* (one substance). In Latin *substantia* means something very different to the English word "substance." For Tertullian, *substantia* was what made something, living or innate, what it is. *Substantia* is the unseen "essence" of something. Later, in fact, the word *substantia* was taken by Latin-speaking theologians as a synonym of the word *essentia* (essence). The Greek-speaking fathers translated the Latin *substantia* by either the word *ousia* (being) or *physis* (nature). For Tertullian, *substantia*, and for the Greek theologians, *ousia/physis*, is what is common to the three divine persons. For them, it is not the origin or cause of anything. The three persons *are* the one substance/being/nature.

The bishops at Nicea in AD 325 and again at Constantinople in AD 381 went one step further; they said in both forms of the one creed that the Father and the Son are *homoousios*/one in being (Latin, *consubtstantia-lis*/consubstantial). The divine three persons not only have in common the one divine *ousia*, they *are* the one *ousia*. Thus, to confess the Father and the Son to be *homoousios* means that the three persons cannot be separated or divided in any way. What they are in unity, they are as persons and vice versa. This confession of the Father and the Son as *homoousios* was an epoch-making objective development in the historical articulation of the doctrine of the Trinity. It said something that Scripture does not say, but all orthodox theologians believe it captures accurately what Scripture implies by calling Jesus "God" and "Lord."

In the middle of the fourth century, the *Homoian* Arians (who believed the Son is *like* in being with the Father) could confess the Son is "God from God," but they could not confess him to be *homoousios* with the Father because as Greek-speaking men they understood this word excluded any separation or division between the Father and the Son and any possibility that what the triune God is in unity, can be other than what each person is in distinction. To confess the Father and the Son as *homoousios* is to say we believe that the Son is God exactly in the same way as the Father, without any caveats. And it is to say we believe that the Father and the Son are not divided in any way; they are the one God. It thus follows that the Father and the Son must be co-eternal and one in majesty, dominion, authority, and glory and they must have one will. No one who eternally subordinates the Son in any way can confess him *homoousios*, once they understand the force of this word.

Their unity of being expressed in the word *homoousios* is not to be thought of impersonally, abstractly or independently of the divine persons. There is no divine being apart from the persons. God's unity is the unique *being-in-communion* of the eternal Father, Son, and Holy Spirit.

For some years after the council of Nicea, Athanasius did not insist on the term *homoousios* because the Arians said they could not accept it since the Bible did not speak of the Father-Son relationship using this word. This was the reason they gave, but the primary reason, the one that meant they could never accept this word, was, as I have just said, that it excluded any separating or dividing of the Father and the Son. However, as the conflict continued and developed Athanasius came to see that this term was needed if Arianism in its different forms, all arguing for the eternal subordination of the Son in some way, was to be absolutely excluded.

Once it had been agreed that the Father and the Son are *homoousios* (one in being), it is of no surprise to find the pro-Nicene fathers, beginning with Athanasius, speaking of the mutual indwelling of the three divine persons and appealing to Jesus' words, "I am in the Father and the Father is in me" in support (John 14:11; 17:21–22). Later the term *perichoresis* was used of this mutual indwelling or coinherence of the three divine persons.[21] The concept of mutual indwelling and the word *perichōrēsis* also exclude any separating or dividing of the Father, Son, and Spirit.

Before leaving this discussion we need to point out that nowhere in the Bible are the Father and the Son said to be *homoousios*. If nothing can be taught doctrinally without explicit and direct biblical support then this foundational Nicene confession would not be binding. This is the logic of claiming that for evangelicals nothing need be believed if it does not have explicit textual support. For Athanasius, and the orthodox theologians who followed him across the ages, and for confessional evangelicals today, this is not the case. Once the church has agreed that this confession captures what Scripture implies—even demands—then we are bound to believe this. We believe it because we agree the word *homoousios accurately* enshrines what Scripture implies. David Yeago makes this point well. He says,

> The ancient theologians were right to hold that Nicene *homoou-
> sios* is neither imposed *on* the New Testament texts, nor distantly

---

21. It is a mistake to take this word to imply dancing together. Etymologically the parts of this word could be taken to imply this but this is not the meaning of the word and this meaning cannot be accepted because it would imply tritheism; three individuals dancing together.

deduced *from* the text, but rather, describes a pattern of judgements *in* the texts, in the texture of scriptural discourse concerning Jesus and the God of Israel.[22]

6. The three divine persons work inseparably

The Scriptures associate distinctive works with each divine person, for example, the Father creation, the Son salvation, and the Spirit sanctification and empowerment for ministry, yet they also make clear that the divine persons always work *as one*. In the Bible, no divine act, work, or operation is ever depicted as the work of one divine person in isolation from the other two. The three persons baptise as one (Matt 28:19), bless as one (2 Cor 13:13), and minister through believers as one (1 Cor 12:4–6). Creation is a work of God involving the Father, Son, and Spirit (Gen 1:1; Pss 36:6; 104:30; John 1:2–3; Col 1:16; Heb 1:10), so too is election (Matt 11:27; John 3:3–9; 6:70; 13:18; Acts 1:2; Rom 8:29; Eph 1:4, 1 Pet 1:2). And so too is salvation (John 3:1–6; Rom 8:1–30; 2 Cor 2:6; Eph 1:3–14). When it comes to divine rule, both the Father and the Son are named "Lord," the supreme ruler, and it would seem also the Holy Spirit (2 Cor 3:17). In the Book of Revelation, the Father and the Son rule from the one throne (Rev 5:13; 7:10). And on the last day, judgment is exercised by God the Father and God the Son (Pss 7:8; 9:7–8; Rom 2:16; Rev 16:7; Matt 25:31–32; John 5:27; Acts 10:42; Phil 2:10).

As far as the Father and the Son are concerned, Jesus himself affirms the doctrine of inseparable operations. He says, "For whatever the Father does the Son does likewise" (John 5:19).

On the basis of this scriptural teaching Athanasius and the Cappadocians concluded that the three divine persons always work as one. Augustine was more explicit. He spoke of the "inseparable" works or operations of the triune persons.[23] His teaching on this matter is accurately summed up in the principle, "the external works of the Trinity are indivisible" (Latin, *opera trinitatis ad extra indivisa sunt*).[24]

However, we should also recognize that the doctrine of inseparable operations is also predicated on a dogmatic basis. Once it was agreed that

22. Yeago, "The New Testament and the Nicene Dogma," 88.

23. Augustine, *The Trinity*, 1.2. 7 (p. 70); 2.1.3 (p. 99).

24. This quote faithfully reflects Augustine's theology, but the exact wording of this principle is found first in medieval Latin theologians.

the Father and the Son are *homoousios* (one in being), separating or dividing the Father and the Son in any way, is excluded on principle. If the Father and the Son, and by inference the Holy Spirit, are the one God then they cannot each work independently.

7. The three divine persons have the one will

In John's Gospel, the incarnate Son does the Father's will (John 4:34; 5:30; 6:38–39, etc.), but the evangelist never suggests that Jesus is under compulsion to do as the Father commands. Rather, John thinks of Jesus as the "instrument or expression of the Father's will."[25] The word obedience is never used in connection with the Father-Son relationship in John's Gospel.

At first thought, the account of Jesus' struggle in prayer in the Garden of Gethsemane (Mark 14:32–42; pars Matt 26:36–46; Luke 22:40–46; cf. John 12:27; Heb 5:7–8) could be taken to indicate that the Father and the Son each will independently. To understand this story rightly a distinction has to be made between the incarnate life of the Son in the economy (history) and his life with the Father and the Spirit in eternity. As fully God and fully man, the incarnate Son has his own human will. In the Garden of Gethsemane, we see the human will of the Son struggling with doing the will of the Father. And so he prays, "Abba, Father, for you all things are possible; remove this cup from me, yet not what I will, but what you will" (Mark 12:36). He asks for his Father's help as the incarnate Son to do his Father's will, despite his fear of the suffering this would entail.

John's more theological account eliminates any suggestion of a clash of divine wills between the Son and the Father. In the Fourth Gospel, Jesus prays a rather different prayer just before his arrest. "Now my soul is troubled. And should I say—'Father, save me from this hour?' No, it is for this reason that I have come to this hour" (John 12:27). This prayer is a declaration by the incarnate Son that his will is to do the Father's will. We see no struggle in these words between the human and the divine will in the incarnate Son, or between the Son's will and that of his Father. What Jesus prays perfectly matches the way John the evangelist speaks of the Father-Son relationship throughout his Gospel. The incarnate Son does the Father's will because he and the Father are "one" (John 10:30; 17:21). The Son wills, acts, and speaks in perfect unison with the Father.

---

25. So, Thompson, *The Promise of the Father,* 150, who exactly follows Basil on this matter.

On basis of this Johannine teaching, the Greek pro-Nicene fathers came to speak of the divine persons willing as one, which Augustine took to mean they have one will.[26] This belief also has a dogmatic basis. If the three divine persons are the one God, they must have one will. This theological inference is now also an essential element in trinitarian orthodoxy.

To argue that the three divine persons each have their own will is to breach divine unity. It implies three Gods, the error called "tritheism." This is why any "social doctrine" of the Trinity that teaches that each divine person has his own will cannot be reconciled with the Nicene faith and must be rejected

8. The three divine persons rule as one

If the Father, the Son, and the Holy Spirit are alike God without any qualifications, then they are alike omnipotent. Omnipotence arguably is the most self-defining of all God's attributes; what makes God God. He alone has sovereign power over all things. To confess that the Father, the Son, and the Spirit are each "Lord" is to acknowledge that they are all omnipotent. In reply to the Arian claim that the Son is eternally set under the Father's authority, the confession "Jesus is Lord" (Acts 2:21; Rom 9:10, 13; 1 Cor 12:3; Phil 2:11, etc.), basic to Christian identity, is the reply. If Jesus is Lord, then he is not set under anyone. The full import of this title is seen when we observe that New Testament writers take texts concerning God from the Greek translation of the Old Testament, which rendered the divine name YHWH as *kurios* (Lord), and apply them to Jesus (Rom 10:13; 1 Cor 1:31; 10:26; 2 Cor 10:17; etc. Cf. Acts 2:21). This transference of the name of God to Jesus is most clearly illustrated in eschatological texts. In the Old Testament, the day when *YHWH* comes in judgment at the end is called "the day of the Lord." In the New Testament, the eschatological climax, "the day of the Lord," is when "our Lord Jesus Christ" comes in judgment (1 Thess 5:23; 4:15–17; 1 Cor 1:7–8; 4:1–5; etc.). Similarly, in Philippians 2:9–11, in speaking of the Son's post-Easter exaltation, Paul says that every knee will bow before him "to the glory of God the Father." These words reflect Isaiah 45:23, a text that envisages the universal worship *of YHWH*.

Unambiguous affirmations that Jesus Christ is God in all might, majesty, and authority are common in the epistle to the Colossians. Christ is said to be "the image" (*eikon*) of the invisible God," and "the firstborn of all

26. Augustine, *The Trinity*, 2.9 (p. 103).

creation" (*prototokos*) (Col 1:15). The latter is an allusion is to Psalm 89:27 where God says of the Messianic King, "I will make him the firstborn, the highest of the kings of the earth." "The firstborn" of the king in Israel shares the honor and rule of the king. Then Paul says that "in him [Christ] all things in heaven and on earth were created" (Col 1:16). The preposition "in" indicates that Christ is the co-creator, not merely the Father's deputy in creating. He has "first place in everything" (Col 1:8). This is so because "in him all the fullness of God was pleased to dwell" (Col 1:20; 2:9), and "he is the head of every ruler and authority" (Col 2:10). Following on in chapter 3 Paul takes up one of the most important Christological motifs in the New Testament. He speaks of the exalted Christ as "seated at the right hand of God" (Col 3:1). These words reflect Psalm 110:1, the most often quoted Old Testament text in the New Testament. This imagery places Jesus Christ "in a position of supreme authority."[27] In the epistle to Hebrews and in the book of Revelation, the imagery changes; the Father and the Son rule from the *one* throne "forever and ever" (Heb 1:8; Rev 5:13; 7:10–12; 11:15).

In John's Gospel, rather than the Son or the Son and the Spirit deferring to the Father, we find a pattern of mutual deference. The Son glorifies the Father (John 7:18; 17:4), and the Father and the Spirit glorify the Son (John 8:50, 54; 12:23; 16:14; 17:1). John also says that before his incarnation the Son shared the Father's glory as his only Son (John 1:14; 12:41; 17:5, 24), during his ministry he revealed the Father's glory (John 1:14; 8:54; 11:4; 13:32; 17:15, 10, 22), and after his glorification on the cross he will again share the Father's glory, a glory he had before the world existed (John 17:5). Thus, trinitarian orthodoxy rightly says, the Father, the Son, and the Spirit are "one in glory."

In the New Testament, the "reign"/"rule" (*basileia*), the "power" (*dunamis*), and the "authority" (*exousia*) of the exalted Christ speak of one reality. Christ now *reigns* as the divine Lord in all *power* (omnipotence), having "all *authority* in heaven and on earth" (Matt 28:19). On this basis, the pro-Nicene fathers spoke of the *monarchia*, the one or united rule of the triune God.[28] In contrast, the Arians limited the *monarchia* to the Father; any authority the Son has is derived authority.[29] The one rule or

---

27. O'Brien, *Colossians and Philemon*, 163.

28. Athanasius, "Defence of the Nicene Definition," 5.26 (p. 167) and, "Councils of Arimium and Seleucia," 26 (p. 463); Basil, "On the Spirit," 45 (p. 28); Gregory of Nyssa, "Against Eunomius," 1.36 (p. 84), etc.

29. This is explicitly spelled out in Eunomius' "Confession of Faith." See Hanson, *The Search for the Christian Doctrine of God*, 619–21.

monarchia of the triune God should not be confused with the pro-Nicene fathers' teaching that the Father is the one source or origin—in Greek, *mia archē*—of the Son, an idea that follows from speaking of the Father as the eternal begetter of the Son.[30]

For the pro-Nicene fathers, the three divine persons are one in being *and* power/authority/reign/dominion; these are two sides of the one coin. For the Arians, the three divine persons are not one in being and thus not one in power/authority/reign/dominion. They are hierarchically ordered in being *and* power; the Son and the Spirit are subordinate to the Father. Following the pro-Nicene fathers, and making the point explicitly, virtually all the Reformation and post-Reformation confessions speak of the three divine persons as one in being/essence *and* power/authority.[31] Following them, the Evangelical Theological Society's doctrinal basis makes the same affirmation. The Father, Son, and Spirit are "one in essence, equal in power and glory."

9. The divine three persons' relations in eternity and operations in the world are ordered

Although the three divine persons are the one God, working inseparably with one will, their life is ordered; how they relate to each other and how they operate follow a consistent pattern that is unchanging and irreversible. This reminds us that nothing is random or arbitrary in God. This *order* in divine life is seen in many ways. For example, and most importantly, there is a processional order. The Father begets the Son and breathes out the Spirit in eternity and sends them both into the world in time.

How God works in the world, however, also follows a consistent pattern. God the Father creates *through* God the Son (Col 1:16, John 1:3; Heb 1:2); judges *through* the Son (Rom 2:16); justifies sinners *through* the Son (Rom 5:1, 21; cf. 1 Theses 5:9), elects to salvation *through* the Son (Eph 1:5); reconciles *through* the Son (2 Cor 5:18; Col 1:20), and he pours out the Spirit *through* the Son (Titus 3:6). Christians come to God the Father *through* God the Son. They thank God the Father *through* God the Son (Rom 1:8; 7:25;

30. See on this, Giles, "The Father as the *Mia Archē*."

31. So the Augsburg confession of 1530, the Belgic confession of 1561, the Thirty-Nine Articles of the Church of England, the Westminster confession of 1646, the London Baptist confession of 1689, and the Methodist articles of 1784. In this usage the terms "power" and "authority" are synonyms, as are "being," "essence," and "nature."

Col 3:17), glorify God the Father *through* God the Son (Rom 16:27), and have access to God the Father *through* God the Son (Eph 2:18).

In the New Testament, as already mentioned, in more than seventy passages the three divine persons are associated together. In these triadic verses, the Father is named first twenty-nine times, the Son first twenty-nine times, and Spirit first seventeen times. These passages indicate that order in divine life it is not to be understood as a hierarchical order; the Father is not always "first," the Son "second," and the Spirit "third." Ranking or hierarchically ordering the three divine persons in any way introduces the Arian error. The Athanasian Creed emphatically excludes hierarchical ordering. It says that in this Trinity "none is before or after, greater or lesser, all are co-equal."

10. The Son in taking human flesh subordinated himself for our salvation

Now we come to a profound objective advance in the development in history of the doctrine of the Trinity; the enunciation of a hermeneutical rule that allowed the Bible to speak with one voice and exclude Arianism in all its forms.

In the Bible there are texts that explicitly speak of the Son as God and the Lord and identify him with YHWH, and yet there are other texts that speak of him as "sent" by the Father (John 8:42; 17:3, 23, etc.), praying to the Father (Mark 14:36; 17:22, etc.), dependent on the Father (Mark 14:36; John 5:19; 8:28; 1 Cor 3:23; Heb 5:7, etc.), obedient to the Father (Rom 5:19; Phil 2:8; Heb 5:8, etc.), and even of him as "less than the Father" (John 14:28). Explaining how these texts can all be affirmed *and* reconciled with texts that speak of the Son as God and the Lord has caused more theological division in the church over the centuries than any other dispute over the Trinity.

Looking back now we can see why the two sides in the debates over the Trinity in the fourth century came to diametrically opposed beliefs as to what the Bible was teaching on the Son. They came to Scripture with irreconcilable presuppositions that led to irreconcilable theological positions. All the Arians believed God must be one, a monad. To be the cause of all things God had to be unitary in an absolute sense. This premise was shared by philosophical Greeks, Jews, and the church fathers of the second century. Thus, Jesus Christ could not be God in the same way as God the

Father. *Assuming this presupposition* they read and interpreted the Bible in this light and found much in support for this belief. None could deny the Bible said God is one and much in the New Testament they thought taught that Jesus Christ, the Son of God, was God in second degree. He is said to be sent by God the Father, he prays to the Father, he does the Father's will, and Proverbs 8:22 says explicitly, "the Lord created me at the beginning of his work," speaking of divine Wisdom, identified with Jesus Christ by the New Testament writers (1 Cor 1:24, 30, etc.). This one text they quoted *ad infinitum.* It proved for them that the Son was created in time and thus subordinate God. In addition, they argued that if Jesus is a "son", he must like all sons be created in time and subject to his father. As "Bible-believing Christians," what they believed seemed to be what Scripture taught.

In contrast, Athanasius, and the later pro-Nicene fathers, came to Scripture with other presuppositions. They believed that the Son is God because in Scripture he is confessed as "the Lord" and as "God"; the church had for three centuries worshiped him as God, and all the great teachers of the church in the first three hundred years of church history had confessed him to be God. Given these presuppositions they were convinced the one God is the Father, the Son, and the Holy Spirit; God for all eternity is triune. The question then became for them, how could the texts that spoke of or implied the subordination of the Son be explained? Thank God Athanasius, with his first-class mind and an unequalled grasp of Scripture, was there to deal with this question.

He argued that Scripture itself gave the answer. He said John 1:1 and 14, and more clearly, Philippians 2:4–11, spoke of "a double account of the Savior," one as God in all might, majesty, and power and one of God in the "form of a servant"—*self-subordinated* God. On this basis, all texts that spoke of or implied the Son's subordination spoke of his *incarnate ministry* in the economy (in history). Proverbs 8:22 was not obviously covered by this rule and Athanasius found this Arian proof text difficult. He gave far more time seeking to explain this one text than any other. His solution was that, read in the light of the whole "scope" of Scripture, Proverbs 8:22 must refer to God's creative act in the historical conception of the Son of God by Mary, not his eternal origins. In this case, his undisclosed hermeneutic was this: one text that seemed to contradict what is basic to Scripture—namely Jesus Christ, the Son of God, is God—could not be interpreted to say otherwise than what Scripture makes the most fundamental truth; the Son is God without any caveats. He is not a creature. The Arian argument based on an analogy between the human father-son relationship and the divine Father-Son relationship, Athanasius found much easier to rebut. For him, creaturely sonship does not and cannot define divine sonship. It is the Bible that should determine our understanding of Jesus as the Son. In the New Testament, the title Son speaks of Jesus as the messianic ruler.

Postulating this "double account" of the Son in Scripture, Athanasius was able to give the church a hermeneutical rule that made sense of all of Scripture and guaranteed the full divinity of the Son, our Lord and Savior. What this rule lays down as a hermeneutical principle has been followed by all catholic theologians across the centuries, is that not everything said of the Son in the New Testament can be read back into his triune life in eternity. Some comments relate only to his self-chosen temporal subordination in his coming down from heaven and to the limitations he accepted in becoming fully man for our salvation. This rule demands that we make a contrast between the Son's earthly ministry "in the form of a servant," what Reformed theologians call, his "state of humiliation," and his heavenly reign as Lord and King, in all might, majesty, and authority, what Reformed theologians call his "state of exaltation."

Modern day complementarians who reject this rule fall into the same error as the Arians. They read the subordination of the Son seen in the economy back into the immanent Trinity. In doing this they commonly appeal to what is called "Rahner's Rule," "*The 'economic' Trinity is the 'immanent' Trinity and the 'immanent' Trinity is the 'economic' Trinity.*"[32] Why they so enthusiastically embraced this rule given by a liberal Roman Catholic; a rule he never explains; a rule that virtually no two theologians can agree to its meaning, and a rule that contradicts the hermeneutic of orthodoxy, raises huge questions. Leaving these questions unanswered I simply point out that the common complementarian interpretation of "Rahner's rule" is tendentious at best and completely mistaken at worst. Whatever Rahner meant by this rule, and no two theologians can agree on this, he is definitely not laying down a hermeneutic on how to faithfully read Scripture on the Son. This is an issue that he does not consider. To read his "rule" in this way is invalid. What then is Rahner saying in his "rule"? I suggest he is simply saying rightly that *just as God is triune in eternity so he is triune in history and vice versa.*

In the previous chapter, I said that *affirming the authority of Scripture is the easy part. How Scripture informs theology is the hard part.* I have

32. Rahner, *The Trinity*, 22, 34.

now illustrated this point. Arius and Athanasius had the same high view of Scripture and both appealed to Scripture for proof of their theological convictions about the Son, but one was right and one wrong. Athanasius was judged to be right because he brought to light the fact that theology is far more than quoting texts and giving "our" interpretation of them. In coming to Scripture, in "doing" theology, we need to think long and hard about what is primary and foundational in Scripture on the issue in focus, how seemingly contradictory comments relate to one another, and, given a question that has arisen since the canon was closed, what in Scripture might point to the answer?

Alister McGrath concludes that Arius got the Bible wrong because of his "proof-text" approach to "doing" theology. He says,

> One of the outcomes of the Arian controversy was the recognition of the futility, even theological illegitimacy, of "proof-texting"— the simplistic practice of believing that a theological debate can be settled by quoting a few passages from the Bible.[33]

Athanasius got it right, says McGrath, because he looked for "The overall pattern disclosed by these texts."[34]

11. The Trinity is not our social agenda

I conclude this account of how the doctrine of the Trinity was developed in the early church, which is also a summary of the Nicene doctrine of the Trinity, by noting a contrast between then and now on one important matter.

The Pro-Nicene fathers gave themselves to establishing a doctrine of the Trinity that honored Christ as God in all might, majesty, and power, predicated on what Scripture explicitly taught or what could be inferred from Scripture. They had no other agenda. In contrast, many modern theologians have a second agenda; to show how the doctrine of the Trinity has practical application to life, particularly social life. In my reading of the writings of the pro-Nicene theologians of the third and fourth centuries, Aquinas, the Reformers, and theologians before the twentieth century, I have not found any one of them appealing to the Trinity in support for any social agenda on earth. For all of them, living in cultures where some were

33. McGrath, *Heresy*, 143.
34. Ibid., 144.

born to rule and some born to obey, hierarchical social order was assumed to be God-given. None of them ever thought that their "co-equal" doctrine of God called into question the social ordering they knew on earth, which they took for granted.

In contrast, many theologians in the twentieth century, wanting to find practical outcomes for the doctrine of the Trinity, and committed to modern ideas of social equality, have argued that God's life in heaven should direct social life on earth. Those who take this path invariably presume a social doctrine of the Trinity where the three divine persons are analogous to three human persons, each with his own will. Paradoxically, those who want to find practical outcomes for the doctrine of the Trinity have irreconcilable beliefs about the immanent Trinity and thus come to irreconcilable conclusions. Some argue that because the three divine persons are "co-equal" in heaven, as the Athanasian Creed says, then all relationships on earth should be co-equal. Complementarians come to exactly the opposite conclusion; the divine persons in heaven are hierarchically ordered and thus the male-female relationship on earth should be ordered hierarchically. In both cases we must suspect *projection;* what is most important to the theologian is read back into the Trinity and then made prescriptive for life on earth.

No matter what our social agenda may be, any appeal to the Trinity should be categorically rejected. The doctrine of the Trinity is our distinctive Christian doctrine of God, not our social or gender agenda. The Bible never makes divine relations in eternity prescriptive for human relationships on earth. What the Bible asks of disciples of Christ, both men and women, is to exhibit the love of God to others and to give themselves in self-denying sacrificial service and self-subordination like the Lord of glory did in becoming one with us in our humanity and dying on the cross. In other words, the incarnate Christ provides the perfect example of how to live with others on earth.

The complementarian appeal to the Trinity in support of the subordination of women is just wrong-headed. Not only is their hierarchical doctrine of the Trinity excluded by the creeds and confessions of the church, but *how* threefold divine relations in heaven, depicted analogically in exclusively male terms, might prescribe the two-fold male-female relationship on earth cannot be explained cogently. If there is an analogy then it would make threefold relationships or male-male relationships the ideal! This argument is special pleading at its worst.

The creeds and confessions

In this book I have said many times, the creeds and confessions represent the collective mind of the church on what is to be believed and they prescribe how the Scriptures are to be rightly read on the doctrines that they address. They spell out what the overwhelming majority of Christians in past times and today are agreed is orthodoxy. Any one is free to believe otherwise, but they must recognize that what they believe *individually* is not the teaching of the Christian community collectively, past or present. It is an idiosyncratic opinion. And they must recognize that to publicly deny what the creeds and confessions teach on the Trinity indicates that on this doctrine they have put themselves outside of the catholic/universal church.

The creeds and confessions were crafted by very able theologians collectively and as such are not ambiguous. What they say on the doctrine of the Trinity represents the culmination of the work of the best theologians at the point when they were drafted. They codify the advances that have been made in developing this doctrine. They hammer in marking pegs, saying there is no going back from what has now been settled. This is now what "we," the Christian community as a whole, believe the Scriptures teach and what every Christian should believe.

The Nicene Creed

In the fourth century, faced with bitter division over what was to be believed about the Trinity, the church expressed its verdict in creedal statements, the most important being the Nicene Creed, promulgated in 381. This creed definitively spells out what should be believed for more than two billion Christians alive today. It is binding on all Roman Catholic, Eastern Orthodox, Anglican, Lutheran, Presbyterian, and Reformed Christians. These two billion believers agree that anyone who denies what is taught in the Nicene Creed stands outside the catholic faith, and any community of Christians that rejects what the Nicene Creed teaches is by definition a sect of Christianity. On this basis, most Christians do not accept Jehovah's Witnesses as orthodox believers because they cannot confess this creed, even though, like evangelicals, they uphold the inerrancy of Scripture.

In the Nicene Creed the Son is communally confessed in these words. Note the "we"—we Christians:

> We believe in one Lord, Jesus Christ, the only (*monogenēs*) Son of God, eternally begotten (*gennaō*) of the Father, God from God, Light from Light, true God from true God, begotten (*gennaō*) not made, of one being (*homoousios*) with the Father. Through him all things were made. For us and our salvation *he came down from heaven*, by the power of the Spirit he was incarnate of the Virgin Mary, and became man.

In these words, six profound statements about the Son are made:

1. He is the one Lord; like the Father, he is omnipotent God.

2. He is the unique (*monogenēs*) Son of the Father; he is not like any human son.

3. He is eternally begotten of the Father, not created.

4. On the basis of his eternal begetting he is "God from God, Light from Light, true God from true God, one in being with the Father"; without any caveats he is God in the same way as the Father.

5. "All things were made through him"; he is the co-creator, and,

6. "For our salvation he came down from heaven: by the power of the Holy Spirit he was incarnate of the Virgin Mary and became man." In coming down from heaven and becoming man he freely subordinated himself for our salvation.

On the vexed question of the interpretation of 1 Corinthians 15:28, a text to which virtually all subordinationists appeal, the Nicene Creed says, "and his [the Son's] kingdom will have no end." In these words, the Creed with very good biblical support (2 Sam 7:12–16; Isa 9:7; Luke 1:33; 2 Pet 1:11; Rev 7:10–12, 11:15; cf. Eph 1:20) makes the eternal rule of the Son integral to the catholic faith. It excludes one possible interpretation of 1 Corinthians 15:28, namely that the Son's reign is temporally limited. His reign *as the Messiah* certainly concludes at the eschaton, but *not* his rule as God.

What more could be said? The intent of the bishops at Nicea was to exclude all expressions of subordinationism inherent in the Arian position; temporal, ontological, derivative, relational, or eschatological. They did this well and at the same time immutably and eternally differentiated the Father and the Son.[35]

---

35. On this see Cunningham, *These Three Are One*, 112.

The Athanasian Creed

The later "Athanasian" Creed, binding on all Roman Catholics, Anglicans, Lutherans, and most European Reformed Christians, is even more explicit.[36] It reflects closely the doctrine of the Trinity as formulated by Augustine in the first half of the fifth century.[37] In this creed the unity of the divine three is stressed, as is their "co-equality." Their eternal differentiation is predicated solely on their distinctive names and differing origination. Allison in warmly commending the Athanasian Creed, says it expresses "the great *advancement* in this doctrine [of the Trinity] from the early days of the church to the fourth/fifth century."[38] This creed declares that,

> The Godhead of the Father, of the Son, and the Holy Spirit is all one: the glory equal, the majesty co-eternal.

> Such as the Father is, such is the Son, such is the Holy Spirit.

> The Father is almighty, the Son is almighty, the Holy Spirit is almighty. And yet there are not three Almighties: but one Almighty.

> The Father is Lord, the Son is Lord: and the Holy Spirit is Lord. And yet there are not three Lords, but one Lord.

> In this Trinity none is before or after, none is greater or less than another. But the whole three persons are co-eternal and co-equal.

> There is one person of the Father, another of the Son, and another of the Holy Spirit."

> The Father is made of none: neither created nor begotten.

> The Son is of the Father alone: not made, nor created, but begotten.

> The Holy Spirit is of the Father and the Son: neither made, nor created, nor begotten, but proceeding.

A more explicit repudiation of the *eternal* subordination of the Son in being, function, or authority is hard to imagine. J. N. D. Kelly is correct;

36. Bray, "Whosoever Will Be Saved: The Athanasian Creed," 47, says this creed failed to get endorsement by the Westminster Confession of 1646 because doubts were then circulating about its authorship by Athanasius.

37. Composed sometime late in the fifth century in southern Gaul (France). It is first mentioned around 542 by the theologian Caesarius of Arles. In Latin, it is called by the words that begin this confession, *Quicumque vult*, "Whosoever will." It was not called the Athanasian Creed until the ninth century.

38. Allison, *Historical Theology*, 242. Italics added.

in the Athanasian Creed "the dominant idea [is] the perfect equality of the three persons."[39]

The Reformation and post-Reformation confessions

The Reformation and post-Reformation confessions of faith were likewise crafted by first-class theologians, with a masterful knowledge of Scripture, in response to opposing opinions. The Nicene doctrine of the Trinity certainly had its critics at this time. I do not plan to go into much detail on what each of the confessions say on the Trinity because this would take too much time and I would bore you. I simply highlight what they are united in affirming. The wordings of the confessions differ, but the doctrine of the Trinity taught does not.

For the pro-Nicene fathers, if the Father and the Son are one in being, they are one in power and vice versa. The Reformation and post-Reformation confessions of faith make this point by consistently stating that the Father, Son, and Spirit are "one in substance/being/essence/nature *and* power." This is an insurmountable problem for complementarians because they consistently argue the Father and the Son do not have the same authority. Yes, I am aware that they speak only of the Son's eternal subordination in "authority," but this difference in terminology is no more significant than when they change the word "subordination" to "submission." In Greek *dunamis* and *exousia* and in English their translations, "power" and "authority," can be synonyms. In trinitarian discourse they are always synonyms. If the triune God has all authority, he has all power, and vice versa. Thus, to deny that the Father and the Son are *one in authority* is to deny that the Father and the Son *are one in power.*

Now to the confessions

The Augsburg Confession of 1530 article 1, states, "There are three persons in this one divine essence, equal in power and alike eternal."

The Belgic Confession of 1561, article 8, says, "All three [are] co-eternal and co-essential. There is neither first nor last: for they are all three one, in truth, in power, in goodness, and in mercy."

---

39. Kelly, *Athanasian Creed*, 79.

The Second Helvetic Confession of 1566, clause 3, on the Trinity, says the "three persons, [are] consubstantial, coeternal, and coequal," and then condemns "all heresies and heretics who teach that the Son and Holy Spirit are God in name only, and also that there is something created and subservient, or subordinate to another in the Trinity, and that there is something unequal, a greater or a less."

The Thirty-Nine articles of the Church of England of 1563, article 1, states that "in the unity of this Godhead there be three persons, of one substance, power, and eternity."

The Westminster confession of 1646, article 2, says, "in the unity of the Godhead there be three persons, of one substance, power, and eternity."

The 1689 London Baptist confession, chapter 2, paragraph 3, speaks of "three subsistences" who are "one substance, power, and eternity."

The Methodist Articles of Religion of 1784, article 1, say, "In the unity of the Godhead there are three persons, of one substance, power, and eternity."

Significantly, moving to the present, the Evangelical Theological Society in its doctrinal basis follows the confessions, making belief in a Trinity of Father, Son, and Holy Spirit, who are "one in essence, equal in power and glory," binding on its members.

And to sum up

1. The *doctrine* of the Trinity does not spring directly from the pages of Scripture. The *doctrine* of the Trinity, such as given in the Nicene Creed of 381, affirms things no text or texts in the Bible actually say.

2. The *doctrine* of the Trinity was hammered out over the centuries by very competent and godly theologians who had the highest view of Scripture. However, in appealing to Scripture they faced two great challenges, first, the Bible seemed to say contradictory things on the Father-Son relationship and, second, many of the questions they were asked to answer about the Father, the Son, and the Spirit, the Bible did not explicitly answer.

3. Answers nevertheless had to be found. Some early answers to complex questions about the Father-Son relationship did not capture adequately what Scripture said and were rejected when better answers emerged. The Arian controversies raised a new set of questions. In the context

of this prolonged and sharp conflict many questions the Bible did not explicitly address had to be answered. Many of the answers given had no specific textual support, and yet were endorsed by the church because it was agreed that these conclusions followed the trajectory that Scripture set. What convinced the church that these answers were right is that in reading the Scriptures in the light of these theological inferences and conclusions all of Scripture made more sense. In this dynamic communal process, slowly, step by step, the Nicene doctrine of the Trinity was formulated and then codified finally in 381 in the Nicene Creed.

4. What the doctrine of the Trinity asserts in essence is that the God revealed in Scripture is eternally one and yet three co-equal persons. Everything else said afterwards is only an extrapolation of these twin truths.

In telling this story of how the doctrine of the Trinity was hammered out in history we have seen how Scripture, tradition, and reason all play their part in "doing" theology. The great church fathers who formulated the doctrine of the Trinity made the Scriptures their primary source, but not in any simplistic way. They soon realized that there were discordant comments in Scripture on the Father-Son relationship and often they had to answer complex questions that the Scriptures never explicitly addressed. This forced them to infer answers on the basis of what Scripture said.

This is where the contribution of *reason*, enlightened by the Holy Spirit, makes its contribution. Justin, Tertullian, Athanasius, the Cappadocian fathers, Augustine, Aquinas, and Calvin, just to mention some representative names, had first-class intellects. Given these great minds, they were able to find a way to read the diverse and sometimes seemingly contradictory comments in Scripture on the Father-Son relationship, to show how all that Scripture said could be harmonised, and to draw deductions or inferences on the basis of what Scripture said that captured the trajectory that Scripture implied.

What each theologian did was build on the work of those before him, sometimes finding a better answer to a complex question and sometimes simply taking the answer offered further. In this way, the doctrine of the Trinity developed organically and progressively step by step. What later theologians called the trinitarian *tradition* developed and took shape in this process. At the council of Nicea in 325 these beliefs were codified in a creed.

This creed became definitive for those who we call today, "the pro-Nicene fathers"—those who were *for* this creed. Later this creed was polished and a few additions were made in 381, and from this time on it became definitive for all Christians. Later still, the Athanasian Creed defined the doctrine of the Trinity more abstractly and technically. Then in the sixteenth century the Protestant Reformers, building on these documents, spelled out clearly yet again the doctrine of the Trinity. All these documents today tell us what the church has come to agree is the doctrine of the Trinity as it is revealed in Scripture. They are now for us *our* doctrinal tradition, the place where we must begin in doing theology. It is with these beliefs in our minds that we should come to Scripture to see if in fact what has been concluded and confirmed time and time across the centuries still makes the most sense of what is revealed in Scripture. The God revealed in Scripture is the Father, the Son, and the Spirit, one God in three persons.

CHAPTER 5

Where Do We Go from Here?

What we have also learned from the telling of this painful story of the rise and fall of the complementarian doctrine of the Trinity is that the Trinity must not be appealed to as proof of either the egalitarian or complementarian doctrine of the sexes. When this has been done the doctrine of the Trinity has been corrupted and debased. We should agree that the threefold life of God in eternity is *not* a model for human relationships in general or in particular of the man-woman relationship on earth. The inevitable consequence of ignoring this rule, it would seem, is that we read into the Trinity our earthy concerns and then appeal to the Trinity in support of them. In doing so we end up with a God we have imagined, not the God revealed in Scripture. Nowhere is this rule more needed to be kept than in the highly charged issue of the man-woman relationship. The temptations to get God on our side are just too great.

To avoid the dangers appealing to the Trinity as the basis for what we believed about the relationship of the sexes, we must make our starting point in thinking about the Trinity the hard won and repeatedly tested conclusions as to what the Scriptures teach on the Trinity, given in the creeds and confessions of the church. It is to these documents that evangelical and Reformed theologians must return at this time as they seek to articulate afresh the doctrine of the Trinity now that the complementarian hierarchical doctrine of the Trinity has been rejected. What the story of the rise and fall of the complementarian doctrine of the Trinity makes plain is just how disastrous it is when theologians ignore or reject the trinitarian tradition of the church and head off alone. Rejecting and denigrating the doctrinal tradition, Knight, Grudem, Ware, and others, devised a doctrine of the

Trinity that reflected and confirmed what was most important to them, the subordination of women, and then they found texts and human analogies that made their novel doctrine sound "biblical." Coming to Scripture with the wrong presuppositions, they came to wrong conclusions. Those who are now to lead the evangelical and Reformed family back to doctrinal orthodoxy must come to Scripture with the presuppositions given in the creeds and confessions of the church. These are presuppositions worked out by the best of theologians across the centuries, communally endorsed, and found in every age to be sure guides to a right reading of Scripture.

A similar principled methodology is also needed in considering what we should believe as Christians about the man-woman relationship, a matter the fall of the complementarian doctrine of the Trinity has put high on the evangelical agenda again. In this case, the starting point must be the Scriptures. There is no authoritative theological tradition to guide us. No creed or confession has ruled on this question and what theologians in the past said on women perfectly reflected the cultural norms of their day, and was often blatantly misogynistic in nature. In studying the Scriptures on this question we should follow the agreed rules of exegesis; avoid language foreign to the Bible such as "role," and look for the big picture. Proof-texting must be avoided. Denigrating those who differ from us on the *interpretation* of any passage as liberals who do not bow to the authority of Scripture certainly will not help.

I am sure many of my readers would wish I said no more on this highly emotive and divisive issue of the relationship of the sexes, which has torn the evangelical family apart in the last forty years, but this cannot be done at this point of time. Leading complementarian theologians are agreed. The fall of the complementarian doctrine of the Trinity—a doctrine that complementarians claimed was clearly taught in Scripture, and which they made the ultimate basis for the subordination of women—must raise questions about the complementarian doctrine of the sexes. I say this as an evangelical egalitarian, but Carl Trueman, a gender complementarian, comes to the same conclusion. He says the rejection of the complementarian doctrine of the Trinity calls into question the whole complementarian position as it has been expressed in recent decades. I quote him again.

> Complementarianism as currently constructed would seem to be now in crisis. But this is a crisis of its own making—the direct result of the incorrect historical and theological arguments upon which the foremost advocates of the movement have chosen to

build their case and which cannot actually bear the weight being placed upon them.[1]

Liam Goligher, another gender complementarian, likewise makes the point that complementarians need to rethink their position. He says they,

> presume to tell women what they can or cannot say to their husbands, and how many inches longer their hair should be than their husbands! They, like the Pharisees of old, are going beyond Scripture and heaping up burdens to place on believers' backs, and their arguments are slowly descending into farce.[2]

The English complementarian theologian and blogger Andrew Wilson agrees with Trueman that complementarianism is now in "crisis" with the abandonment of the trinitarian argument and, with Goligher, that in detail it often borders on "sheer silliness."[3] For him, like me, he thinks the challenges now before complementarians are all positive. They open up the possibility of a radical rethink of what the Bible actually says on the sexes. He writes,

> Personally, I'm quite optimistic about the fallout from the whole debate. . . . I think correctives are good. I think robust challenges to faulty formulations of doctrine will, in the end, produce health rather than decay. Admittedly there is a certain type of complementarian argument that, in all likelihood, will be either gradually jettisoned, or refined and nuanced until it can no longer be recognised as the same thing, and this, I suspect, is what Carl [Trueman] means by "complementarianism as currently constructed." But the overall effect of that change will be positive, rather than negative, for complementarianism as a whole.[4]

What adds great weight to these calls for a rethink of complementarianism, the most strident voices coming from complementarians, is that before June 2016 the most significant leaders of the complementarian movement argued that their theology stood or fell with their beliefs about the Trinity. The subordination of the Son and the subordination of women were inextricably connected, as 1 Corinthians 11:3 proved, they claimed. Wayne Grudem said for twenty-five years that he believed that how the

---

1. Trueman, "Farenheit 381."
2. Goligher, "Is It Okay?"
3. Wilson, "When Complementarianism 'Slides into Sheer Silliness.'"
4. Wilson, "Complementarianism in Crisis."

Trinity is understood "may well turn out to be the most decisive factor in finally deciding" the bitter debate between evangelicals about what the Bible teaches on the status and ministry of women.[5] Dr. Jared Moore, in his 2015 review of *One God in Three Persons*, written for the Southern Baptist Convention website, says,

> If complementarians can prove that there is a hierarchy in the immanent (ontological) Trinity, *then they win*, for if a hierarchy exists among the Three Persons of God, and these Three Persons are equally God, then surely God can create men and women equal yet with differing roles in the church and home.[6]

Given that the complementarian doctrine of a hierarchically ordered Trinity has now been abandoned, even by leaders of the complementarian movement, and that they have agreed that 1 Corinthians 11:3 neither subordinates the Son nor women, the reality of a major crisis for complementarian theology cannot be denied. Their loss of the civil war over the Trinity means that they cannot avoid a time of reconstruction where they examine afresh what the Scriptures actually teach on the relationship of the sexes, without any appeal to the Trinity.

Fortunately, they have evangelical and Reformed egalitarian friends, holding to the highest view of Scripture, who will gladly sit down with them to recommence the healthy and open discussion on what the Bible teaches on the status and ministry of women that flourished before the Danvers Statement was promulgated in December 1987, claiming to rule authoritatively on what the Bible teaches. With the Trinity now excluded from this discussion, complementarians and evangelical egalitarians have the opportunity to listen and learn from each other for the first time in thirty years after they divided into two hostile opposing camps. The world has moved on from the time that breach occurred. A rethink is needed. Women are now leading in every sphere of life; whipping us men in the education stakes; earning good graduate and postgraduate theological degrees in growing numbers; doing excellent theological work—Aimee Byrd and Rachel Miller illustrate this point, and the happiest and most rewarding marriages are profoundly equal. What is more, evangelical egalitarians have undeniably moved the debate forward light years on what the Bible says on the sexes.[7] The most important of these developments is the

---

5. Grudem, *Evangelical Feminism*, 411, note 12.

6. Moore, "The Complementarians Win."

7. Two books make this assertion incontestable; Payne, *Man and Woman: One in*

growing consensus among Catholic and Protestant biblical scholars that Genesis chapters 1 to 3 do not subordinate women to men before the fall.[8] The Bible makes the fall the point where the man begins to rule over the woman, depicting it as something not good; not the God-given ideal. In listening to egalitarians, complementarians may be surprised to learn that they are not liberals who reject the authority of the Bible, or radical feminists that want overthrow Christian family values. And complementarians may be surprised to find that egalitarian evangelicals wholeheartedly and unreservedly agree with them that God has made us men and women; our maleness and femaleness is God-given and good. We egalitarians are all for gender differentiation. We do not deny it; we affirm it. And for this reason, egalitarians wholeheartedly and unreservedly endorse the complementarity of the sexes. We are agreed; God made us male and female and we need each other to be fully human; to be *complete*.

It seems to me that we have exciting times ahead as complementarians and evangelical egalitarians learn from each in the quest to find a common mind on what the Scriptures teach on the status and ministry of men and women. In this process we can hope that old divisions and misunderstandings that for too long have painfully and sharply divided brothers and sisters in Christ can be resolved and overcome for the sake of the gospel. In agreement with the complementarian Reformed theologian Andrew Wilson,

> I'm quite optimistic about the fallout from the whole debate. . . .
> I think correctives are good. I think robust challenges to faulty formulations of doctrine will, in the end, produce health rather than decay.[9]

Christ, and, Westfall, *Paul and Gender*. I believe my essay, "The Genesis of Equality," also progresses the debate significantly. I point out in this essay that the majority of contemporary Old Testament scholars, Catholic and Protestant, now agree that Genesis 2 does not subordinate woman to man before the fall; the subordination of women is entirely a consequence of the fall. It is thus not the creation ideal; something good. And I argue in this essay that no appeal to an Old Testament text in the New can prescribe the historical meaning of an Old Testament text.

8. I set out the evidence for this assertion in Giles, "The Genesis of Equality."

9. Wilson, "Complementarianism in Crisis."

Bibliography

Allison, Gregg R. *Historical Theology: An Introduction to Christian Doctrine*. Grand Rapids: Zondervan, 2011.

Anatolios, Khaled. *Retrieving Nicaea*. Grand Rapids: Baker, 2011.

Applegate, Kirby, and Scott Horrell. Review of *The Eternal Generation of the Son*, by Kevin N. Giles. *Bibliotheca Sacra*, 172 (2015) 118–20.

Athanasius. "Councils of Arimium and Seleucia." In *The Ante–Nicene Fathers*, vol. 4, edited by A. Roberts and J. Donaldson, 448–80. Reprint. Grand Rapids: Eerdmans, 1985.

———. "Defence of the Nicene Definition". In *The Ante–Nicene Fathers*, vol. 4, edited by A. Roberts and J. Donaldson, 149–72. Reprint. Grand Rapids: Eerdmans, 1985.

———. "Discourses against the Arians." In *The Ante–Nicene Fathers*, vol. 4, edited by A. Roberts and J. Donaldson, 330–447. Reprint. Grand Rapids: Eerdmans, 1985.

Augustine. *The Trinity*. Edited and translated by Edmund Hill. New York: New City, 1991.

Award, N. G. "Should We Dispense with *Sola Scriptura*? Scripture, Tradition and Postmodern Theology." *Dialog* 47.1 (2008) 64–79.

Barth, Karl. *Church Dogmatics*, 1.1. Edited by Geoffrey Bromiley. Edinburgh: T. & T. Clark, 1956.

———. *The Humanity of God*. London: Collins, 1961.

Basil. "On the Spirit." In *The Ante–Nicene Fathers*, vol. 8, edited by A. Roberts and J. Donaldson, 1–50. Reprint. Grand Rapids: Eerdmans, 1985.

Belleville, Linda L. "Son Christology in the New Testament." In *The New Evangelical Subordinationism: Perspectives on the Equality of God the Father and God the Son*, edited by Dennis W. Jowers and W. Wayne House, 59–79. Eugene, OR: Pickwick, 2012.

BIBLE. New Revised Standard Version. Grand Rapids: Zondervan, 1989.

Bilezikian, Gilbert. "Hermeneutical Bungee-Jumping: Subordination in the Godhead." *Journal of the Evangelical Theological Society* 40.1 (1997) 57–68.

Bird, Michael F. *Evangelical Theology: A Biblical and Systematic Introduction*. Grand Rapids: Zondervan, 2013.

———. "Even More on the Complementarian Calvinism Debate on the Trinity." *Patheos*, 12 June 2016. http://www.patheos.com/blogs/euangelion/2016/06/even-more-on-the-complementarian-calvinism-debate-on-the-trinity/

———. "Patristic Scholar Lewis Ayres Weighs in on the Intra-complementarian Debate on the Trinity." *Patheos*, 13 June 2016. http://www.patheos.com/blogs/euangelion/2016/06/patristics-scholar-lewis-ayres-weighs-in-on-the-intra-complementarian-debate/

———. "Patristic scholar Michel R. Barnes Weighs in on the Intra-complementarian Debate on the Trinity." *Patheos*, 12 June 2016. http://www.patheos.com/blogs/euangelion/2016/06/patristics-scholar-michel-r-barnes-weighs-in-on-the-intra-complementarian-debate-on-the-trinity/

Bird, Michael F., and Robert Shillaker. "Subordination in the Trinity and Gender Roles: A Response to Recent Discussions." In *The New Evangelical Subordinationism: Perspectives on the Equality of God the Father and God the Son*, edited by Dennis W. Jowers and W. Wayne House, 288–310. Eugene, OR: Pickwick, 2012.

Blocher, Henri. "The Analogy of Faith in the Study of Scripture." In *The Challenge of Evangelical Theology: Essays in Approach and method*, edited by Nigel M. de S. Cameron, 17–38. Edinburgh: Rutherford House, 1987.

Bray, Gerald R. "Whosoever Will Be Saved: The Athanasian Creed and the Modern Church." In *Evangelicals and the Nicene Faith: Reclaiming the Apostolic Witness*, edited by Timothy George, 45–60. Grand Rapids: Baker, 2011.

Burk, Denny. "My Take-away from the Trinity Debate." *Denny Burk*, 10 August 2016. http://www.dennyburk.com/my-take-aways-from-the-trinity-debate/

———. "Why the Trinity Must Inform Our Views on Gender." *Denny Burk*, 13 August 2013. http://www.dennyburk.com/why-the-trinity-must-inform-our-views-on-gender-roles-ctmagazine.

Butner, D. Glen. "Eternal Functional Subordination and the Problem of the Divine Will." *Journal of the Evangelical Theological Society* 58.1 (2015) 131–50.

Byrd, Aimee. "Another Look at the Bikini Question." *Mortification of Spin*, 5 June 2013. http://www.alliancenet.org/mos/housewife-theologian/another-look-at-the-bikini-question#.WHRFYvB96Um.

———. "John Piper's Advice to Women in the Workplace." *Mortification of Spin*, 17 August 2015. http://www.alliancenet.org/mos/housewife-theologian/john-pipers-advice-for-women-in-the-workforce#.WHRKrvB96Ul.

———. "Reinventing God." *Mortification of Spin*, 6 June 2016. http://www.mortificationofspin.org/mos/housewife-theologian/reinventing-god#.WGG6xPB96Um.

———. "Sanctified Testosterone?" *Mortification of Spin*, 21 April 2016. http://www.alliancenet.org/mos/housewife-theologian/sanctified-testosterone#.WHRMYvB96Ul.

———. "The Spin of Patriarchy." *Mortification of Spin*, 24 September 2014. http://www.alliancenet.org/mos/housewife-theologian/the-spin-of-patriarchy#.WHRFpPB96Ul.

———. The UFC and Femininity." *Mortification of Spin*, 25 February 2013. http://www.alliancenet.org/mos/housewife-theologian/the-ufc-and-femininity#.WHRE__B96Ul.

———. "What Denny Burk Could Do." *Mortification of Spin*, 11 August 2016. http://www.alliancenet.org/mos/housewife-theologian/recovering-from-biblical-manhood-and-womanhood#.WHRLEvB96Ul.

Cary, Phillip. "The New Evangelical Subordinationism." In *The New Evangelical Subordinationism: Perspectives on the Equality of God the Father and God the Son*, edited by Dennis W. Jowers and W. Wayne House, 1–12. Eugene, OR: Pickwick, 2012.

Cassidy, James J. "Kevin Giles: *The Eternal Generation of the Son*." *Reformedforum*, 15 January 2013. http://reformedforum.org/kevin-giles-the-eternal-generation-of-the-son/.

Christians for Biblical Equality. "Statement on Men, Women and Equality." http://www.cbeinternational.org/content/statement-men-women-and-biblical-equality.

Claunch, Kyle. "God is the Head of Christ." In *One God in Three Persons: Unity of Essence, Distinction in Persons, Implications for Life*, edited by Bruce A. Ware and John Starke, 65–94. Wheaton, IL: Crossway, 2015.

Cochrane, Arthur C. *Reformed Confessions of the Sixteenth Century*, London: SCM, 1966.

Cole, Graham. "Trinity without Tiers." *Euangelion*, 21 June 2010. http://euangelizomai.blogspot.com.au/2010/06/trinity-without-tiers-graham-cole.html.

Coppedge, Allan. *The God Who is Triune*. Downers Grove, IL: IVP, 2007.

Cowan, Christopher W. "I Always Do What Please Him." In *One God in Three Persons: Unity of Essence, Distinction in Persons, Implications for Life*, edited by Bruce A. Ware and John Starke, 47–64. Wheaton, IL: Crossway, 2015.

Cullman, Oscar. *The State in the New Testament*. Rev. ed. London: SCM, 1963.

Cunningham, David. *These Three are One: The Practice of Trinitarian Theology*. London: Blackwell, 1998.

Dallaville, Nancy. Review of *The Eternal Generation of the Son*, by Kevin N. Giles. *Theological Studies* 74 (2013) 738–40.

Danker, F. W. *A Greek-English Lexicon of the New Testament and Other Early Christian Literature*. 3rd ed. Chicago: University of Chicago Press, 1979.

Davis, John Jefferson. "Trinity, Gender, and the Ordination of Women: How Complementarians Should *Not* Argue Their Position." *Preserving the Trinity*, 4–7. Minneapolis: CBE International, 2016.

Duncan, J. Ligon. "The Doctrine of the Trinity and Complementarianism in Recent Discussion." *Reformed Theological Seminary*, 12 November 2016. http://subsplash.com/reformtheosem/v/j3waa8e.

Durst Rodrick K. *Reordering the Trinity: Six Movements of God in the New Testament*. Grand Rapids: Kregel, 2015.

East, Brad. Review of *The Eternal Generation of the Son*, by Kevin N. Giles. *Restoration Quarterly* 56.3 (2014) 188–89.

Emmerson, Matthew, and Luke Stamps. "Responding to Bruce Ware with Charitable Criticism." *Biblical Reasoning*, 9 July 2016. https://secundumscripturas.com/2016/07/09/responding-to-bruce-ware-with-charitable-criticism/.

Erickson, Millard. *God in Three Persons: A Contemporary Interpretation of the Trinity*. Grand Rapids: Baker, 1995.

———. *Who's Tampering with the Trinity? An Assessment of the Subordination Debate*. Grand Rapids: Kregel, 2009.

———. "Language, Logic, and the Trinity: A Critical Examination of the Eternal Subordinationist View of the Trinity," *Priscilla Papers*, 31.3 (2017), 8–15.

Fairbairn, Donald. *Life in the Trinity: An Introduction to Theology with the Help of the Church Fathers*. Downers Grove, IL: IVP, 2009.

Frame, John. *The Doctrine of God: A Theology of Lordship*. Phillipsburg, NJ: P & R, 2002.

———. Review comment, *One God in Three Persons*, edited by Bruce Ware and John Starke. https://www.crossway.org/books/one-god-in-three-persons-tpb/.

———. *Systematic Theology: An Introduction to Christian Beliefs*. Phillipsburg, NJ: P & R, 2013.

Franke, John S. *The Character of Theology: An Introduction to its Nature, Task and Purpose*. Grand Rapids: Baker, 2005.

Geisler, Norman. *Systematic Theology*, vol. 2. Minneapolis: Bethany, 2003.

George, Timothy, ed. *God the Holy Trinity*. Grand Rapids: Baker, 2006.

Giles, Kevin. *Better Together: Equality in Christ*. Brunswick East, Australia: Acorn, 2010.

———. *Created Woman: A Fresh Study of Biblical Teaching*. Australian Capital Territory: Acorn, 1985.

———. "Defining the Error Called Subordinationism." *Evangelical Quarterly* 87.3 (2014) 207–24.

———. *The Eternal Generation of the Son: Maintaining Orthodoxy in Trinitarian Theology*. Grand Rapids: Zondervan, 2012.

———. "An Extended Review of *One God in Three Persons: Unity of Essence, Distinction of Persons, Implications for Life*, edited by Bruce Ware and John Starke." *Priscilla Papers* 30.1 (2016) 21–30.

———. "The Father as the *Mia Arche*, the One Originating Source of the Son and the Spirit, and the Trinity as the *Monarchia*, the One Undivided Ruler." *Colloquium* 46.2 (2014) 175–92.

———. "The Genesis of Confusion: How Complementarians Have Corrupted Communication." *Priscilla Papers* 29.1 (2015) 22–29.

———. "The Genesis of Equality." *Priscilla Papers* 28.4 (2014) 3–9.

———. "Is the Son Eternally Submissive to the Father? An Egalitarian-Complementarian Debate." *Christian Research Journal* 31.1 (2008) 11–21.

———. *Jesus and the Father: Modern Evangelicals Reinvent the Doctrine of the Trinity*. Grand Rapids: Zondervan, 2006.

———. "The Orthodox Doctrine of the Trinity; Part 1, the Doctrine in Summary; part 2, Commentary." *Priscilla Papers* 26.3 (2012) 12–23.

———. Review of *Recovering Biblical Manhood and Womanhood: A Response to Biblical Feminism*, edited by Wayne Grudem and John Piper. *Evangelical Quarterly* 65.3 (1993) 276–81.

———. Review of *The Holy Trinity in Scripture, History, Theology and Worship*, by Robert Letham. *Evangelical Quarterly* 78.1 (2006) 85–94.

———. "The Subordination of Christ and the Subordination of Women." In *Discovering Biblical Equality: Complementarity without Hierarchy*, edited by Ronald W. Pierce and Rebecca M. Groothuis, 334–52. Downers Grove, IL: IVP, 2005.

———. *The Trinity and Subordinationism: The Doctrine of God and the Contemporary Gender Debate*. Downers Grove, IL: IVP, 2002.

———. "The Trinity without Tiers." In *The New Evangelical Subordinationism: Perspectives on the Equality of God the Father and God the Son*, edited by Dennis W. Jowers and W. Wayne House, 262–87. Eugene, OR: Pickwick, 2012.

———. *Women and Their Ministry: A Case for Equal Ministries in the Church Today*. Melbourne: Dove Communications, 1977.

———. "The Nicene and Reformed Doctrine of the Trinity," *Priscilla Papers*, 31.3 (2017), 3–7.

Giles, Kevin, and Robert Letham. "An Egalitarian-Complementarian Debate: Is the Son Eternally Submissive to the Father?" *Christian Research Journal* 31.1 (2008) 11–21.

Goligher, Liam. "Is It Okay to Teach Complementarianism Based on Eternal Subordination?" *Mortification of Spin*, 3 June 2016. http://www.alliancenet.org/mos/housewife-theologian/is-it-okay-to-teach-a-complementarianism-based-on-eternal-subordination#.WGGyLfB96Ul

Groothuis, Rebecca Merrill. "Equal in Being Unequal in Role." In *Discovering Biblical Equality: Complementarity without Hierarchy*, edited by Ronald W. Pierce and Rebecca M. Groothuis, 301–54. Downers Grove, IL: IVP, 2005.

Gregory of Nyssa. "Against Eunomius." In *The Ante-Nicene Fathers*, vol. 5, edited by A. Roberts and J. Donaldson, 33–248. Reprint. Grand Rapids: Eerdmans, 1985.

Grenz, Stanley J. *Revisioning Evangelical Theology: A Fresh Agenda for the 21st Century.* Downers Grove, IL: IVP, 1993.

————. *The Social God and the Relational Self: A Trinitarian Theology of the Imago Dei.* Louisville, KY: Westminster John Knox, 2001.

Grenz, Stanley J., and John H. Franke. *Beyond Foundationalism: Shaping Theology in a Postmodern Context.* Louisville, KY: Westminster John Knox, 2001.

Grenz, Stanley J., and Denise M. Kjesbo. *Women in the Church: A Biblical Theology of Women in Ministry.* Grand Rapids: IVP, 1995.

Griggs, Tom. *New Perspectives for Evangelical Theology: Engaging with God, Scripture and the World.* London: Routledge, 2010.

Grudem, Wayne. "Another Thirteen Evangelical Theologians Who Affirm the Eternal Submission of the Son to the Father." *Reformation 21*, 20 June 2016. http://www.reformation21.org/blog/2016/06/another-thirteen-evangelical-t.php.

————. "Appendix 1, The Meaning of *Kephalē* ('Head')." In *Recovering Biblical Manhood and Womanhood: A Response to Biblical Feminism*, edited by Wayne Grudem and John Piper, 425–68. Wheaton, IL: Crossway, 1991.

————. "Biblical Evidence for the Eternal Submission of the Son to the Father." In *The New Evangelical Subordinationism: Perspectives on the Equality of God the Father and God the Son*, edited by Dennis W. Jowers and W. Wayne House, 223–61. Eugene, OR: Pickwick, 2012.

————. *Countering the Claims of Evangelical Feminism.* Colorado Springs: Multnomah, 2006.

————. *Evangelical Feminism and Biblical Truth.* Sisters, OR: Multnomah, 2004.

————. *Evangelical Feminism: A New Path to Liberalism.* Wheaton, IL: Crossway, 2006.

————. "Doctrinal Deviations in Evangelical-Feminist Arguments about the Trinity." In *One God in Three Persons: Unity of Essence, Distinction in Persons, Implications for Life*, edited by Bruce A. Ware and John Starke, 17–46. Wheaton, IL: Crossway, 2015.

————. *Systematic Theology: An Introduction to Biblical Doctrine.* Downers Grove, IL: IVP, 1994.

————. "Whose Position Is Really New?" *CBM.Org.* http://cbmw.org/public-square/whose-position-on-the-trinity-is-really-new/.

Grudem, Wayne, and John Piper, eds. *Recovering Biblical Manhood and Womanhood: A Response to Biblical Feminism.* Wheaton, IL: Crossway, 1991.

Gundry, Stanley E. "An Evangelical Statement on the Trinity." *Priscilla Papers* 25.4 (2011) 12–13.

Haddad, Mimi, ed. *Preserving the Trinity.* Minneapolis: CBE International, 2016.

Hall, Christopher. *Reading Scripture with the Church Fathers*. Downers Grove, IL: IVP, 1988.

Hamilton, James. "That God May Be All in All." In *One God in Three Persons: Unity of Essence, Distinction in Persons, Implications for Life*, edited by Bruce A. Ware and John Starke, 95–108. Wheaton, IL: Crossway, 2015.

Hanson, Collin. "Anathemas All Around." *Christianity Today*, 10 October 2008. http://www.christianitytoday.com/ct/2008/octoberweb-only/141–53.0.html.

Hanson, Richard P. C. *The Search for the Christian Doctrine of God*. Edinburgh: T. & T. Clark, 1988.

Hatch, Nathan. "*Sola Scriptura and Novus Ordo Seclorum*." in Nathan Hatch and Mark Knoll, editors, *The Bible in America: Essays in Cultural History*, New York: Oxford, 1982.

Hill, Wesley, *Paul and the Trinity: Persons, Relations, and the Pauline Letters*. Grand Rapids: Eerdmans, 2015.

Holmes, Stephen. *The Holy Trinity: Understanding God's Life*. Milton Keynes, UK: Paternoster, 2012.

———. "Reflections on a New Defence of 'Complementarianism.'" 22 May 2015. http://steverholmes.org.uk/blog/?p=7507.

———. "Stephen Holmes Rejoinder." In *The Holy Trinity Revisited: Essays in Response to Stephen Holmes*, edited by Thomas A. Noble, and Jason S. Sexton, 137–55. Milton Keynes, UK: Paternoster, 2015.

Horton, Michael S. "The Eternal Generation of the Son: Maintaining Orthodoxy in Trinitarian Theology by Kevin Giles." *White Horse Inn*, 31 October 2014. https://www.whitehorseinn.org/article/the-eternal-generation-of-the-son-maintaining-orthodoxy-in-trinitarian-theology-by-kevin-n-giles/.

Irons, Lee. "*Monogenēs* in the Church Fathers: A Response to Kevin Giles." *The Upper Register*, 1 January 2017. http://upper-register.typepad.com/blog/2017/01/monogenes-in-the-church-fathers-a-response-to-kevin-giles-part-5.html.

Jewett, Paul. *Man as Male and Female*. Grand Rapids: Eerdmans, 1975.

Johnson, Keith E. "Augustine's Trinitarian Reading of John 5: A Model for the Theological Interpretation of Scripture." *Journal of the Evangelical Theological Society* 52.4 (2009) 799–811.

———. "Trinitarian Agency and the Eternal Subordination of the Son: An Augustinian Perspective." *Themelios* 36.1 (2010) 7–25.

Jones, Mark. "Eternal Subordination of Wills? Nein." *New City Times*, 13 June 2016. https://newcitytimes.com/news/story/wayne-grudems-historical-theology; https://newcitytimes.com/news/story/eternal-subordination-of-wills-nein.

———. "The Irony of Mohler's Post on the Trinity." *New City Times*, 29 June 2016. https://newcitytimes.com/news/story/mohler-on-the-heresy-of-three-wills.

Jowers, Dennis W. "The Inconceivability of Subordination with a Simple God." In *The New Evangelical Subordinationism: Perspectives on the Equality of God the Father and God the Son*, edited by Dennis W. Jowers and W. Wayne House, 375–410. Eugene, OR: Pickwick, 2012.

Jowers, Dennis W., and W. Wayne House, eds. *The New Evangelical Subordinationism: Perspectives on the Equality of God the Father and God the Son*. Eugene, OR: Pickwick, 2012.

Karkkainen, Veli-Matti. The *Trinity: Global Perspectives*. Louisville, KY: Westminster/John Knox, 2007.

Kaiser, Walter. "Hermeneutics and the Theological Task." *Trinity Journal* 12.1 (1991) 3–14.

Kassian, Mary, and Nancy L. Moss. *True Woman 101: Divine Design*. Chicago: Moody, 2012.

Kuyper, Abraham. *Principles of Sacred Theology*. Grand Rapids: Baker, 1980.

Keener, Craig S. *The Gospel of John: A Commentary*. Peabody, MA: Hendrickson, 2003.

Keller, Tim. *The Reasons for God: Belief in an Age of Skepticism*. London: Dutton-Penguin, 2008.

Kelly, Douglas. *Systematic Theology: Grounded in Holy Scripture and Understood in the Light of the Church*. Fearn, UK: Mentor, 2008.

Kelly, J. N. D. *The Athanasian Creed*. London: A & C Black, 1964.

Knight, George W. *The New Testament Teaching on the Role Relationship of Men and Women*, Grand Rapids: Baker, 1977.

Letham, Robert. "Eternal Generation in the Church Fathers." In *One God in Three Persons: Unity of Essence, Distinction in Persons, Implications for Life*, edited by Bruce A. Ware and John Starke, 109–26. Wheaton, IL: Crossway, 2015.

———. *The Holy Trinity in Scripture, History, Theology and Worship*. Phillipsburg, NJ: P & R, 2004.

———. "Reply to Kevin Giles." *Evangelical Quarterly* 80.4 (2008) 339–45.

Letham, Robert, and Kevin Giles. "An Egalitarian-Complementarian Debate: Is the Son Eternally Submissive to the Father?" *Christian Research Journal* 31.1 (2008) 11–21.

Leupp, Roderick T. *The Renewal of Trinitarian Theology*. Downers Grove, IL: IVP, 2008.

Linblad, Stefan. "Stefan Linblad Replies to Bruce Ware." *Mortification of Spin*, 8 July 2016. http://www.alliancenet.org/mos/1517/stefan-lindblad-responds-to-bruce-ware#.WHyVTvB96Ul.

Lindgren, Caleb. "From Proxy War to Civil War." 16 June 2016. http://www.christianitytoday.com/ct/2016/june-web-only/gender-trinity-proxy-war-civil-war-eternal-subordination.html

Lints, Richard. *The Fabric of Theology: A Prolegomena to Evangelical Theology*. Grand Rapids: Eerdmans, 1993.

McCall, Tom. "Gender and the Trinity Once More." *Trinity Journal* 36NS (2015) 263–80.

McGrath, Alister E. *Genesis of Doctrine*. Oxford: Blackwell, 1990.

———. *Heresy: A History of Defending the Truth*. New York: HarperOne, 2009.

———. *Studies in Doctrine*. Grand Rapids: Zondervan, 1997.

———. *Understanding the Trinity*. Eastbourne, UK: Kingsway, 1990.

McKnight, Scot M. "The Battle Rumbles Along: The Trinity of Complementarians." *Jesus Creed*, 10 June 2016. http://www.patheos.com/blogs/jesuscreed/2016/06/10/the-battle-rumbles-along/.

———. "Kevin Giles—The ETS Response to Grudem and Ware." 23 November 2016. http://www.patheos.com/blogs/jesuscreed/2016/11/23/kevin-giles-the-ets-response-to-grudem-and-ware/.

Macleod, Donald. "Subordinationism (Out of the Blue)." http://www.donaldmacleod.org.uk/dm/subordinationism-out-of-the-blue/.

Miller, Rachel. "Continuing Down This Path Complementarians Lose." *A Daughter of the Reformation*, 22 May 2015. https://adaughterofthereformation.wordpress.com/2015/05/22/continuing-down-this-path-complementarians-lose/.

———. "Does the Son Eternally Submit to the Father." *A Daughter of the Reformation*, 28 May 2015. https://adaughterofthereformation.wordpress.com/2015/05/28/does-the-son-eternally-submit-to-the-authority-of-the-father/.

————. "Grudem and Ware Double Down on the Eternal Subordination of the Son." *A Daughter of the Reformation*, 10 December 2016. https://adaughterofthereformation.wordpress.com/2016/12/10/grudem-and-ware-double-down-on-the-eternal-subordination-of-the-son/

————. "Is Complementarian Just Another Name for Patriarchy?" *A Daughter of the Reformation*, 29 September 2014. https://adaughterofthereformation.wordpress.com/2014/09/29/is-complementarian-just-another-word-for-patriarchy/.

————. "True Woman 101 Divine Design." *A Daughter of the Reformation*, 8 May 2015. https://adaughterofthereformation.wordpress.com/2015/05/08/true-woman-101-divine-design/.

————. "What's Wrong with Biblical Patriarchy?" *A Daughter of the Reformation*, 31 May 2012. https://adaughterofthereformation.wordpress.com/2012/05/31/whats-wrong-with-biblical-patriarchy/.

Mohler, Albert. "Humility and Heresy—Lesson from a Current Controversy." *Albert Mohler*. 6 June 2016. shttp://www.albertmohler.com/2016/06/28/heresy/

Moore, Jared. "The Complementarians Win: A Review of *One God in Three Persons*." 19 May 2015. http://sbcvoices.com/the-complementarians-win-a-review-of-one-god-in-three-persons/.

Neuer, Werner. *Man and Woman in Christian Perspective*. Translated by Gordon Wenham. London: Hodder and Stoughton, 1981.

"New Calvinism." *Wikipedia*. https://en.wikipedia.org/wiki/New_Calvinism; http://www.newcalvinist.com/.

O'Brien, Peter. *Colossians and Philemon*. Waco, TX: Word, 1982.

O'Reilly, Matthew P. Review of *The Eternal Generation of the Son*, by Kevin N. Giles. *Reviews in Religion and Theology* 20.2 (2013) 218–21.

Oberman, Heiko. *The Harvest of Medieval Theology*. Cambridge: Harvard University Press, 1963.

Oliphint, Jared. "John Pipers Twelve Features of the New Calvinism." *Reformation Today*, 17 May 2014. http://reformedforum.org/john-pipers-twelve-features-new-calvinism/.

Olson, Roger E. "Thoughts about Another Evangelical Controversy." *Patheos*, 12 March 2012. http://www.patheos.com/blogs/rogereolson/2012/03/thoughts-about-another-evangelical-controversy/.

Olson, Roger E., and Christopher A. Hall. *The Trinity*. Grand Rapids: Eerdmans, 2002.

Ovey, Michael J. "True Sonship—Where Dignity and Submission Meet." In *One God in Three Persons: Unity of Essence, Distinction in Persons, Implications for Life*, edited by Bruce A. Ware and John Starke, 127–54. Wheaton, IL: Crossway, 2015.

————. *Your Will be Done: Exploring Eternal Subordination, Divine Monarchy and Divine Humility*. Oxford: Latimer Trust, 2016.

Payne, Philip B. *Man and Woman, One in Christ: An Exegetical and Theological Study of Paul's Letters*. Grand Rapids: Zondervan, 2009.

Peppard, M. "Adopted and Begotten Sons of God: Paul and John on Divine Sonship." *Catholic Biblical Quarterly* 73.1 (2011) 92–110.

Pierce, Ronald W., and Rebecca, M. Groothius, eds. *Discovering Biblical Equality: Complementarity without Hierarchy*. Downers Grove, IL: IVP, 2005.

Pruitt, Todd, "A mythological Godhead," July 9, 2016, http://www.alliancenet.org/mos/1517/a-mythological-godhead#.WRkDoO6GOUk

Rahner, Karl. *The Trinity*. Translated by J. Donceel. London: Burns and Oates, 1997.

Reissig, Courtney. "Why Complementarian Men Need Complementarian Women." *Christianity Today*, June 2016. http://www.christianitytoday.com/women/2016/june/why-complementarian-men-need-complementarian-women.html.

Reymond, Robert L. *A New Systematic Theology of the Christian Faith*. Nashville: Thomas Nelson, 1998.

Sanders, Fred. "Generations Eternal and Current." *The Scriptorum Daily*, 1 June, 2015. http://scriptoriumdaily.com/generations-eternal-and-current/

————. "A Plain Account of Trinity and Gender." 17 June 2016. http://scriptoriumdaily.com/a-plain-account-of-trinity-and-gender/.

————. *The Triune God*. Grand Rapids: Zondervan, 2016.

Scanzoni Letha D., and Nancy A Hardesty. *All We're Meant to Be: Biblical Feminism for Today*. Grand Rapids: Eerdmans, 1974.

Shellnutt, Kate. "The Complementarian Women behind the Trinity Issue." *Christianity Today*, 22 August 2016. http://www.christianitytoday.com/ct/2016/september/behind-trinity-tussle.html.

Stackhouse, John. G. ed. *Evangelical Futures: A Conversation on Theological Method*. Grand Rapids, Baker, 2000.

Stamps, Luke. Review of *The Eternal Generation of the Son*, by Kevin N. Giles. *Journal of the Evangelical Theological Society* 59.4 (2017) 878–81.

Starke, John. "Augustine and His Interpreters." In *One God in Three Persons: Unity of Essence, Distinction in Persons, Implications for Life*, edited by Bruce A. Ware and John Starke, 155–73. Wheaton, IL: Crossway, 2015.

Storms, Sam. Review comment, *One God in Three Persons*. https://www.crossway.org/books/one-god-in-three-persons-tpb/

Strachan, Owen, and Gavin Peacock. *The Grand Design: Male and Female He Made Them*. Fearn, UK: Christian Focus, 2016.

Swain, Scott. "God from God, Light from Light: Retrieving the Doctrine of Eternal Generation." http://subsplash.com/reformtheosem/v/aktvufb.

The Danvers Statement. http://cbmw.org/uncategorized/the-danvers-statement/.

Thompson, Marianne M. *The Promise of the Father: Jesus and God in the New Testament*. Louisville, KY: Westminster, 2000.

Thompson, Thomas. Review of *The Eternal Generation of the Son* by Kevin Giles. *Augustinian Studies* 44.2 (2013) 289–92.

Trier, Daniel J., and David Lauber, eds. *Trinitarian Theology for the Church*. Downers Grove, IL: IVP, 2009.

Trueman, Carl, and Todd Pruitt. "An Accidental Feminist." *Mortification of Spin*, 18 August 2015. http://www.alliancenet.org/mos/postcards-from-palookaville/an-accidental-feminist#.WHScoPB96Ukhttps://www.firstthings.com/blogs/firstthoughts/2015/09/on-gender-differences-and-evangelical-complementarianism.

————. *The Creedal Imperative*. Wheaton, IL: Crossway, 2012.

————. "Fahrenheit 381." *Mortification of Spin*, 7 June 2016. http://www.mortificationofspin.org/mos/postcards-from-palookaville/fahrenheit-381.

————. "Motivated by Feminism? A Response to Recent Criticism." *Mortification of Spin*, 14 June 2016. http://www.alliancenet.org/mos/postcards-from-palookaville/motivated-by-feminism-a-response-to-a-recent-criticism#.WFuMRvB96Um.

————. "What the Church Can Do." *Mortification of Spin*, 23 July 2013. http://info.alliancenet.org/mos/podcast/what-church-do#.WHShKvB96Uk.

van Leeuwen, Mary Stewart. *Sword between the Sexes: C. S. Lewis and the Gender Debate*. Grand Rapids: Brazos, 2010.

Vanhoozer, Kevin. *The Drama of Doctrine: A Canonical Linguistic Approach to Christian Theology*. Louisville, KY: Westminster/John Knox, 2005.

Ware Bruce A. *Father, Son, and Holy Spirit: Relationships, Roles, and Relevance*. Wheaton, IL: Crossway, 2005.

———. "God the Son—At Once Eternally God with his Father, and Eternally Son of the Father." *Reformation 21*, 9 June 2016. http://www.reformation21.org/blog/2016/06/god-the-sonat-once-eternally-g.php.

Ware, Bruce A., and John Starke. *One God in Three Persons: Unity of Essence, Distinction in Persons, Implications for Life*. Wheaton, IL: Crossway, 2015.

Warfield, Benjamin B. "The Idea of Systematic Theology." In *Studies in Theology*, 49–90. New York: Oxford, 1932.

Westfall, Cynthia Long. *Paul and Gender: Reclaiming the Apostle's Vision for Men and Women in Christ*. Baker: Grand Rapids, 2016.

Williams, Daniel H. *Evangelicals and Tradition: The Formative Influence of the Early Church*. Grand Rapids Baker, 2005.

———. *Retrieving the Tradition and Renewing Evangelicalism: A Primer for Suspicious Protestants*. Grand Rapids: Eerdmans, 1999.

———, ed. *Tradition, Scripture, and Interpretation: A Sourcebook of the Ancient Church*. Grand Rapids: Baker, 2006.

Williams, E. S. "The New Calvinists part I." 4 July 2012. http://www.newcalvinist.com/who-are-the-new-calvinists-part-1/.

Wilson, Andrew. "When Complementarianism Slides into Silliness." *Think Theology*, 9 September 2015. http://thinktheology.co.uk/blog/article/when_complementarianism_gets_silly.

———. "Complementarianism in Crisis." *Thinking Theology*, 6 July 2016. http://thinktheology.co.uk/blog/article/complementarianism_in_crisis.

Witherington, Ben. "The Eternal Subordination of Christ and Women." *Ben Witherington*, 22 March 2006. http://benwitherington.blogspot.com.au/2006/03/eternal-subordination-of-christ-and-of.html.

———. "Kevin Giles on the Trinity." *Patheos*, 5 December 2016. http://www.patheos.com/blogs/bibleandculture/2016/12/05/kevin-giles-on-the-trinity/.

Woods, Mark. "Wayne Grudem Has Changed His Mind on the Trinity—Just Not Enough Say His Critics." *Christian Today*, 1 June 2016. http://www.christiantoday.com/article/wayne.grudem.has.changed.his.mind.on.the.trinity.just.not.enough.say.critics/102617.htm.

Yarnell, Malcolm B. *God the Trinity: Biblical Portraits*. Nashville: B & H Academic, 2016.

Yeago, David. "The New Testament and the Nicene Dogma: A Contribution to the Recovery of Theological Exegesis." In *The Theological Interpretation of Scripture*, edited by Stephen Fowl, 87–100. Oxford: Blackwell, 1997.

Author Index

Subject Index

Made in the USA
Monee, IL
24 March 2024